NEW LIFE, NO SEX, What Now?

Straight Talk About Sex and Celibacy

YOLANDA HARRIS

Illustrations by Daniel Thomas.

Please note that Evangelista Media's™ publishing style does not capitalize the name satan and related names. We choose not to acknowledge him, even to the point of violating grammatical rules.

DEDICATION

This book is dedicated to women who struggle with sexual frustration, sexual immorality, and fornication, and those who are crying out to God for help with the celibacy walk. Satan wants to keep us bound by sin but God wants a brighter future for us.

The Word says:

> *For the wages of sin is death, but the gift of God is eternal life in Christ Jesus our Lord* (Romans 6:23).

> *...Jesus* [is] *the author and finisher of our faith...* (Hebrews 12:2).

I pray that you allow these words to be your light in times of darkness and a helping hand stretched out to assist you when you need it most. You can't do anything more or anything less to change the *awesome love* God has for you today.

Your yesterday no longer matters. Just move forward with God and He will take you into a destiny you cannot begin to imagine. For it is written that He "is able to do *exceedingly abundantly above* all that we ask or think, according to the power that works in us..." (Eph. 3:20). If you are in Christ Jesus, that power is in you. God says, "Just wait on Me."

> *Those who wait on the Lord shall renew their strength; they shall mount up with wings like eagles, they shall run and not be weary, they shall walk and not faint* (Isaiah 40:31).

Take these words to heart, and allow them to change your life forever.

Acknowledgments

I would like to first acknowledge the author of this book and my life: my Daddy, God. God, you have used me to create a work for You and I am truly honored. I pray that I have made You proud. You are everything to me. When I felt like I had no one, You were always there for me. I am overjoyed to call You Daddy. You are the source of my "holy high."

Just as more than half of the New Testament was written by Paul under the inspiration of the Holy Spirit, this book is written by me, under the Spirit's inspiration.

To my Madison, Mommy loves you very much. Everything I do, I do for you. This is a journey I pray you go through smoothly. Know that Mommy is always here for you; that will never change. Keep a pair of sunglasses handy because your future is bright!

Thank you to my Faith Christian Center family in Smyrna, Georgia for the teaching and direction that has revealed who I am in God. I've learned so much in the year and a half that I have been a member. There are no words to express how grateful I am.

I want to say a *huge* thank you to my parents, Art Wallace and Denise Wallace, and my spiritual parents, Craig and Valerie Washington, and everyone I call family. You all have been an important part of my life. God has orchestrated these divine connections and I couldn't have asked for a better set of families.

Thank you to my illustrator, Daniell Thomas. You envisioned what I was speaking and put it to paper. You are a very talented individual. I know that God is about to turn your life upside down, in the most pos-itive way. Get ready because your future is beautiful.

I would like to give a BIG thanks to the ones who heard from God and were obedient to His leading—my publishing team, Evangelista Media. I know God spoke to you because this has truly been a fast-paced process. Thank you for being so patient with me and adhering to as many changes as I had. I pray that God gives you a hundredfold return for all your labor that you have put into this project. Partnering with you guys has truly been an amazing experience and from the depths of my heart, I thank you.

I want to say a special thank you to the nine ladies who helped make this book possible. Thank you for allowing me to understand your deep-est thoughts. Know that your efforts will not go unnoticed. God has chosen you to be a part of this movement. Your stories will help ladies all over the world who need that female bond to get to their next level.

Last, but definitely not least, I want to thank my husband. Although, in the natural, I haven't met you yet, I know that you are out there and I choose to stay celibate for our future. God is my head, but soon you will be my head. "For the husband is head of the wife, as also Christ is head of the church; and He is the Savior of the body" (Eph. 5:23). I look for-ward to meeting you and starting our journey into marriage together.

Endorsements

I have read books on celibacy and the importance of waiting. This book gave more than just information; it has the Word of God to accompany and bring peace to any celibacy issue. I was able to relate to one of the young women in the story and take the journey with her. Yolanda Harris definitely has the passion to spread the love of God to His baby girls. It's a must-read for everyone.

Niako Hanzy
Founder, Destined Designs

Reading the Introduction alone, one can see that this book was written to meet the needs of women in different places in their lives and thoughts toward celibacy. Everyone's journey is different. Yet, having a book with nine unique stories gives readers an opportunity to connect and allow God to speak through the lives of others.

Brenda Grimes

Life is a journey, and this book will take you on one through the lives of other women. I am certain you will find yourself identifying with them. *Insightful* and *inspiring* are the best words I can use to describe the end result of reading this book. Not only are you getting real stories, but you are getting practical notes on real-life situations. This book is a must-read for everyone, no matter the journey or background. Everyone can take away something they didn't have before.

Samara Gonzalez

But those who wait on the Lord shall renew their strength; they shall mount up on wings like eagles, they shall run and not be weary, they shall walk and not faint.

—Isaiah 40:31

Contents

FOREWORD

In the twenty-first century, sex and the yielding to its covert and overt devices has not only crippled the Body of Christ but has also crippled our families, communities, nation, and our human race. The promotion of sex through television and all social media outlets provides a daily diet of lustful, lascivious, and licentious practices.

There are rare moments in history when someone is brave enough and courageous enough to attack the concept, principles, and practice of celibacy. Yolanda Harris has joined the ranks of the "Brave Hearts" of the world. Her book, if read and applied, will give women, men, boys, and girls another Christ-centered tool to use in their journey to hold on.

Every season, someone is birthed in the kingdom of God who dares to step out of the proverbial "religious box." Sister Yolanda Harris is next on God's list of New Guard ministers to be birthed for this season and this generation. Many New Guard ministers sit quietly in the maternity wards of the kingdom of God, awaiting their turn to bring forth fresh, out-of-the-box revelation.

This book, written by our Sister Harris, is not only out of the box; it will crush every religious box concerning sex, celibacy, and the need to hold on. Over the past few years we have watched Yolanda not only blossom into a mature Christian, but exhibit the very lifestyle she writes about.

Many pastors have a difficult time discussing sex, celibacy, and holding on from the pulpit. This is why God has to use undercover agents not on the stage of Christendom to reach a generation of unmarried Christians. Sister Yolanda's book will not only reach the heart of every single person trying to live the celibate life; it will reach and become an app, if you will, for pastors and churches.

Fresh ideas, fresh approaches, and fresh revelation are what God's people are seeking and are desperately in need of. The testimonies in this book will inspire and ignite a celibacy movement/revolution that will spread like wildfire through a social networking generation.

New Life, No Sex, What Now? will bring into practice the Law of Spiritual Reproduction described Second Timothy 2:2:

> *And the [instructions] which you have heard from me along with many witnesses, transmit and entrust [as a deposit] to reliable and faithful men who will be competent and qualified to teach others also* (AMP).

Holy Ghost dominoes will be the ultimate result with a book such as this one. I know and pray that God will be glorified through this book; that those who buy and read it will be edified; and that the devil will be horrified at those who make a decision to put the principles into practice.

My wife and I endorse this book with all our heart, mind, and soul. We look forward to hearing the many stories about lives that will be changed because of it.

Thank you, Sister Yolanda Harris, for daring to be who God called you to be.

Much love,
Your Spiritual Mom and Dad

Rev. Craig and Valerie Washington

Preface: To Pastors

I am well known in the singles community within my church. Some even call me Momma Yo. I say that to say this: the majority of churches today are filled with singles, and the singles in your church need this book.

Not many singles talk about their sexual relationships, not because they don't have them, but because they don't think others are fighting the same battle they are. Many may talk to friends who are still "in the world," asking them for advice about something God has created to be only between a husband and a wife. They are asking advice from the wrong people.

If the singles within your church are not talking to you or to counselors within the church, then they are talking to someone else. That someone may be a negative influence. Singles need to know that they are not alone on this journey. It's not a journey they can travel alone. We need to promote accountability within the singles community. We also need to let them know that this journey can be a success, if they walk hand in hand with God.

If you are not educating your singles on the topic of sex and its true meaning, what are you waiting for? You need to tend to your flock, before the wolf in sheep's clothing does (see Matt. 7:15; John 10:11-12).

Introduction

Have you ever sat around and questioned this thing called *celibacy*? Have you asked yourself, "What is it all about? Why should I be celibate, anyway? I mean, instant gratification is so much better than waiting—*right?*"

So many women struggle with this very issue. Even women of faith deal with it. In our day, celibacy is seen as the road less traveled. But why? Why aren't more people willing to abstain from sex until after marriage?

It is true that, in a world full of lust and temptation, celibacy is not an easy goal to reach. For many people, having sex is like picking out what to wear to work. They don't realize that the after effects of sex could be as serious as death, for it is written: "the wages of sin is death…" (Rom. 6:23).

It is so important to understand that sex was designed to be enjoyed in the confines of marriage between a man and a woman (see Mark 10:6-12). Yes, it is a battle every day to kill the flesh and live according to the Spirit. The flesh will always want to do the opposite of what the Spirit wants. That's why we have to renew our minds to follow Christ every day (see Rom. 12:2).

We must remember that we are spirit beings who live in a body and possess a soul (see 1 Thess. 5:23). If we have our spirit man and our minds focused on the same thing, our bodies will find it hard to make our decisions for us. Instead, our bodies will follow the spirit man within.

Nine Lives, Nine Journeys

This is a journey taken through the lives of nine single Christian women who have chosen the path of celibacy. You will receive an in-depth view of what they have to say: about the good days and bad days, about strong urges, about the thin line between what is sin and what isn't, and much more.

God always speaks to us about our sin; the only question is whether we want to hear what He was to say. A lot of the time, we don't. We want to do what our flesh dictates and then consult God after the consequences have set in. We know that He can still work every situation out for good, because He's God (see Rom. 8:28). But what He wants for us is His very best. The thing is that we have to want it ourselves.

For this journey, you will need a checklist. Whatever we women go through in life, we usually have a checklist associated with it. It notes the tasks we need to complete in order to feel that we have accomplished something.

The road to celibacy is no different. A checklist is required because it allows you to focus on specific tasks that will keep you on the path without falling. The nine personal stories you are about to read are like nine different developmental stages. If you utilize their checklists, they will ensure that you will not fall.

Remember that these real-life stories reveal nine individual paths to celibacy. While names have been changed for the sake of privacy, the people are real. The first letter of each of their names is stylized for a reason: they spell out the word *sanctuary*. The nine women whose stories you are about to read have left the past behind and entered the sanctuary—a life with God at the center.

Remember, as you read, that it is written: "Judge not, that you be not judged" (Matt. 7:1). I love how *The Message* version breaks this verse down. It says: "Don't pick on people, jump on their failures, criticize their faults—unless, of course, you want the same treatment."

Keep this in mind as you read the women's stories and witness their faults. Like all of us, they have flaws; but they also have made major accomplishments. With the help of God, they are progressing to this day.

Now that you know where we are going, put on your sneakers and get ready to hike, as we travel on this road called *celibacy*.

A Note to Readers

You will notice that each story includes a word in stylized capital letters that represents a fruit of the Spirit. There are nine fruits listed in Galatians 5:22-23. They are love, joy, peace, longsuffering, kindness, goodness, faithfulness, gentleness, and self-control. These women are operating in the fruit of the Spirit because the Spirit of Christ dwells in their hearts.

Mount
Instant Gratification

The road to instant gratification starts off as an easy, sweat less, and what seems like an effortless road. It doesn't take much energy and the path to get to Mt. Instant gratification is quick. But the coming down from the mountain will be long, hard, and will require much effort on your part. It will leave you with a lot of cuts (emotional ties), scaring (disappointments), and bruising (broken hearts) that can easily be seen (internal hurt showing up externally). It will also take a long time to heal (healing of a broken heart and broken spirit).

ABANDONMENT

Where do I start? How do I begin?
Trying to find a way, to put these emotions to an end—
Emotions of loneliness and a lot of built-up hurt,
How are you still affecting me, when you're six feet in the dirt?
I thought I could get over it, I mean it's been so many years.
Now I have issues with men, and abandonment is what I fear.
Will I ever find someone who will want to stay and
Find out who I really am, and how I got this way?
Never had anyone that I could depend on.
One minute they're here, and the next minute they're gone.
Father of Mine was given at birth,
But No-Good Dad is how you left this earth.
I wish you were there, to take me to school,
And beat my butt, when I broke the rules;
To tell me I was pretty, and I was Daddy's little girl,
To say that without me, you couldn't live in this world.
To punish me when I was bad, and say, "It'll be alright,"
When I had my first date, that didn't go so right.
To take me to a dance, where it was Daddy and me,
Looked at by the other dads, as what they wanted to be;
To be there when I had my daughter, and hold her in your hands,
Whispering to her the secrets of how to find a good man.
Walking me down the aisle, when it was the right time,
Making a toast on my behalf, while raising your glass of wine.
That's the dad I wanted, but I guess with my luck
I got stuck with the no-good dad, who didn't give a what.
The dad who came around only when someone died,
And questions about child support only brought about lies.
Had a whole other family that I didn't know,

Decided when she was seven, it was time for you to show—
Show me I had a sister, another child I see.
Wonder if you're a better father to her, than you are with me.
She sees you all the time, taking trips to the park,
And teaching her to ride her bike, until the moment it gets dark.
Must be nice to have another, and leave one behind,
But I guess it's cool with me, because I've turned out just fine.
Yeah, I've got emotional issues, thanks to good ole you;
Repressed them for so long, now, I don't know what to do.
You tried to make amends, right before you died,
Nope, it didn't work; I guess you can say you tried.
Even in death you hurt me, because you forgot my name,
Didn't mention me in the will…nothing for me to claim.
Mom said I should fight it, and get what's mine,
But you never gave me anything alive, so, no, I'll be just fine.
I'll continue to live my life, as if you weren't there,
Make amends with your family, cause, just maybe, they care.
I have a daughter now, and from there you can probably see
I'm trying to make sure her father doesn't do her like you did me.
I used to write about you, and all I could do was cry,
But as I write this one, my eyes are surprisingly dry.
Maybe it's because I've cried enough for today,
Wishing these things on paper, were words that I could say.
But you are gone now, never to come back again
And these are emotions that I'm trying to put to an end.
So, fathers, take care of your girls; be the best you can be
Or I promise they will grow up to be just like me.

(Written before coming to Christ)

Chapter 1

SHARI:

LOVE, SEX, AND RELATIONSHIPS

BUT I'M WORTHY OF SO MUCH MORE!

"For I know the thoughts and plans that I have for you, says the Lord, thoughts and plans for welfare and peace and not for evil, to give you hope in your final outcome. Then you will call upon Me, and you will come and pray to Me, and I will hear and heed you. Then you will seek Me, inquire for, and require Me [as a vital necessity] and find Me when you search for Me with all your heart" (Jeremiah 29:11-13 AMP).

My Story

Love, sex, and relationships—yes, that is what my life was all about. Although I had plenty of distorted relationships and sex, it was *LOVE* that was lacking most. I didn't know what it was or how to obtain it; but I knew it was missing in my life.

My name is Shari. I grew up without my parents, both of whom were on the streets, addicted to drugs and alcohol. As a result, my sister and I were bounced around from orphanage to orphanage, and from house to house. It was madness, at least until my grandmother got custody of us.

When I was seven, my father was killed. If that wasn't bad enough, my mother was killed eight years later, and my sister decided to move out on her own. That left me alone with my grandmother. I had no purpose in life and felt like "black girl lost."

Because of these events, I never learned what real love was; but I was determined to find it. At the age of sixteen, I had sex for the first time. That's when I started to relate sex with love and security.

I was the textbook example of someone looking for love in all the wrong places. At first sex provided temporary fulfillment. It later developed into a source of financial security. I had men who wanted to spend time with me, take me to dinner, and pay my bills. I didn't have to worry about anything. They bought my food, paid my rent, bought me cars, and made sure I had money in my pocket. Everything was taken care of—but at what cost?

I was trying to fill a void with what my heart and mind craved: attention. Attention from men was what I loved, especially when they started spending money on me. I became a money-hungry man eater. As long as men gave me what I wanted, I didn't care what they were doing in the streets. They thought they were using me. Little did they know that I was using them, too. So, it was a win/win situation, or at least I thought it was.

Boy, was I wrong.

I thought I was doing them dirty, but God showed me that I was doing myself dirty. First Corinthians 6:18 says that "he who commits sexual immorality sins against his own body." I was sinning against myself.

These are the things I'm learning now. Until two years ago, I didn't understand why I was looking for fulfillment in all the wrong places. But by the grace of God, I can see it now. He has revealed these things to me, and the healing process has begun.

Celibacy has been part of that process. I am twenty-six years old and have been on this celibacy journey for two months now. I don't feel as though I've made a full commitment yet, but that doesn't mean I want to be double-minded (see James 1:6-8).

The closer I get to God, the more guilty and uncomfortable I feel regarding sex. The more I learn about the importance of celibacy and of not fornicating, the less I feel myself desiring sex. The reason I say I haven't fully committed is because of the way I'm handling relationships. Instead of having the conversation I need to have—admitting that I have made a covenant with God—I just reject phone calls. My approach has been one of avoidance more than commitment.

It's just awkward, really. There's a guy I have been seeing for a while; and we still hang out and go to the movies and such. Every time we talk, I tell him I'm about to go to Bible study or to church. I don't feel he has fully accepted my decision, because even after I gave him "the talk" about my walk with Christ, we kept having sex.

I think he felt that what I was saying and what I was doing were two different things. Matthew 5:37 says, "Let your 'Yes' be 'Yes,' and your 'No,' 'No.' For whatever is more than these is from the evil one." My walk didn't match my talk. If my words and actions were in alignment, he would have taken me more seriously.

Things are not perfect, but I am getting it all in order now. Six months ago, when I got saved, my attitude was: "I'm going to focus on what God has for me, but I'll just ignore the part about fornication."

The truth is, I wasn't praying about that part of my life at first. Once I started going to God about it, He began dealing with me. As I asked Him for answers, He revealed the truth, just like He says: "Ask, and it will be given to you…" (Matt. 7:7).

Little by little, I started feeling all the guilt, shame, and pain that went along with sex. I realized that I was only hurting myself with my disobedience. Now, I see celibacy as a form of obedience that unlocks all the power and blessings that God has for me!

Deuteronomy 28:1-2 explains how obedience works:

Now it shall come to pass, if you diligently obey the voice of the Lord your God, to observe carefully all His commandments which I command you today, that the Lord your God will set you high above all nations of the earth. And all these blessings shall come upon you and overtake you, because you obey the voice of the Lord your God…

I realize that I have to get to the point where I consistently reverence God through my body. There are several ways to reverence Him, including through praise, singing, and tithing. But the best way I can reverence God is by keeping my body pure.

During the past six months, I have felt like I'm in boot camp. It's as if God is tearing me down so He can build me back up again. He is helping me by identifying the issues from my past that are affecting my present. The journey is amazing, although I still don't feel like I have committed myself fully. I do spend time reading, praying, and going to church, but I know it's not enough. It will never be enough if I am not applying and *doing* what the Word says, instead of just *hearing* it (see James 1:22).

What good is knowledge, if you don't use it? It's like God is saying that I am walking around like a smart dumb girl, sitting in class popping my gum and texting on my phone instead of answering the questions the teacher is asking me. I have all the answers; I'm just not applying what I have learned.

God has shown me that He has so much more for me. He has shown me a great circle of guys who I call my brothers in Christ. Watching them proves that there are guys out there who openly worship Christ and have good character. I'm in awe of each of them, but God is showing me that the person He has for me will encompass all of their best qualities put together. All I have to do is wait on God's best for me, and just slow myself down.

So, as I continue on this celibacy journey, I will continue to be honest with myself, always praying and listening to God. As Scripture says: "This Book of the Law shall not depart from your mouth, but you shall meditate in it day and night…" (Josh. 1:8).

It is a matter of committing myself to everything my heavenly Father has for me. I don't want to have one foot in heaven and one in hell. I don't want to be hot and cold. I don't want to be a hearer and not a doer. I don't want to be the one who goes to church on Sunday morning and the club on Sunday night. The church is filled with those types of people, but I don't want to be one of them. God has told me that I am not one of them. He has told me that He has so much in store for me, but it's not happening as quickly as it should because of my disobedience.

I'm still in awe of how He works, especially because everything is so new to me. I'm at the place where I'm listening to and recognizing His voice. This leads me to where I am listening to and trusting what He says, because I am one of His sheep (see John 10:27). Still, I am insecure about trusting myself; I know that I am F.O.A. (Fresh Off the Altar). But I also know that it will only get better with time.

Boundaries

There are many boundaries that people can set for themselves, but from my experience these are the ones helping me on my journey:

- No dating. God is definitely working on me! I need to allow Him time to heal the internal hurts I am going through. I read an article about a woman who took a year off. For that year, it was just her and God. I don't know what time frame God has in mind for me, but I know I really need it. For however long it is, I will be building my strength and endurance to fight temptation, and learning what this covenant and commitment with God really means. If anyone expresses an interest in dating me, I will tell him up front that I am not dating anyone at this time. I want to remove any hidden agendas men might bring my way.

- Keep boundaries around social media. I need to be sure I'm not spending so much time on the social networks that I forsake my time alone with God. He should be my main focus, not what people are doing and saying on Facebook.

- Limit my time within my small-group Bible study. I need to go to Bible study and then fellowship afterward for about thirty minutes only. I need to be comfortable being with just me. God has told me that He has given me support because I asked for it; but right now, all I need is Him. When times get hard, I have people to call, but they can't walk this walk for me.

- Keep out of worldly situations and things from my past. In the beginning of my walk, I was still drinking. I wasn't a big drinker, but I would have a glass of wine. Then those feelings would creep in. It let me know that I shouldn't drink anymore. I don't need to put myself in any situations where I may be tempted.

Advice

There are many women on this journey and some who want to begin the journey, but you must first realize that you are worthy. You are worthy of all the love that God has for you.

Throughout my life, I felt unworthy. Some of the things that I went through, no woman or child of God should ever have to go through. These are things I wouldn't wish on my worst enemy. I have had to realize that God has so much more for me.

I started to feel as though this was my life and this was going to be my life; but God has other plans for me. When I first came back to church, in my first membership class, a lady walked up to me and said, "Stop feeling as though you are not worthy."

Right then, I knew God had placed me at this church for a reason. She said, "You are so worthy of God's love, and you don't have to do anything to receive it. The love that He has for you now is the love that He will have for the rest of your life. No matter what you may do in life, He will still love you just like He loves you right now."

She continued to explain that she needed to tell me that. God used her to give me the message of LOVE that He had been trying to convey to me all along. She used the exact same word—*unworthy*—that I used to describe what I'd felt all my life.

At that very moment, I was able to tap into all the reasons I felt unworthy. I had to realize that God chose me. I accepted Him, but He *chose* me ("before the foundation of the world," according to Ephesians 1:4). Although I was still worried about my past, God wasn't. He told me that He doesn't call the righteous; He calls the sinner and that's why He called unto me.

So, His message was for me to stop worrying about my past. It's called *a past* for a reason. It will stay in the past as long as I leave it there. The apostle Paul learned the same lesson, and wrote:

> *Brethren, I do not count myself to have apprehended; but one thing I do, forgetting those things which are behind and reaching forward to those things which are ahead…* (Philippians 3:13).

Just know that we are all entitled to God's blessings. No matter what you have done, He will not hold anything against you. "There is…no condemnation to those who are in Christ Jesus, who do not walk according to the flesh, but according to the Spirit" (Rom. 8:1).

He is not going to take away the potential blessing He designed specifically for you, just because of something you have done in your past. Give God a chance and watch Him do what He does best—which is show up and show out. It works every time.

Know that sex is not love. God is love. I heard someone say, "If a man can wait for you, that's a beautiful thing. As badly as God wants that for you, you should want it for yourself." God knows what He's doing and He sets His commandments and standards for us because He knows what's best for us.

Do you want to accept God's best or the world's mediocrity…its leftovers?

Shari's "No Sex, What's Next?" Checklist

- Spend time alone with God.

- Know that you are worthy of His love.

- No matter what your past looks like, move forward to your future with God.

- Leave the past in the past.

- Concentrate on the fact that God is love. Sex is not love.

- If you are living with someone (a man not your husband) move out on your own; God will provide.

- Learn from every situation you face.

- Know your boundaries and stick with them.

Get to know who *you* are.

Message from God

You, My child, are worthy—worthy of My riches and glory. Nothing will I withhold from you. I call you blessed. I am the same yesterday, today, and forevermore. I don't change. But you, My child, can change. I will provide that change in you. There's nothing that you can do to make Me love you any more or any less. You are My child, and you are fearfully and wonderfully made. Know that everything I make is good. You are no exception. While your physical parents may have passed on, I am your Shepherd. I am still here for you and I will continue to guide you to all truth. Just cast your cares on Me and know that I am the great I AM. You can do all things through Me because I strengthen you. You are My seed and the fruit of the womb is a reward. You are My reward. Because you are a partaker in Christ, you receive everything that Christ receives. All the riches and all the glory are yours, My child. Always remember that My Word never comes back to Me void, so if I said it, know that it will come to pass; for I am not a man that I should lie.

Chapter 2

ᴀbbey:

I Want to Touch Myself...

But God Won't Be Pleased

"Shun immorality and all sexual looseness [flee from impurity in thought, word, or deed]. Any other sin which a man commits is one outside the body, but he who commits sexual immorality sins against his own body" (1 Corinthians 6:18 AMP).

My Story

Purity is an instruction from God. I'm doing it because He asked me to. If it were up to me and my feelings, I would have continued having sex. I can't say it has always been that way, because I did not always enjoy sex. For physical reasons, it was a struggle; but I thought that, for a man to stick around, I had to give him what he wanted. I know now that my mentality wasn't best for me. I didn't know the *Joy* of being in God—but He soon showed me!

My name is Abbey. I'm twenty-one, and I've been celibate for six months. During that time I've heard people's stories about growing up without a father, and all the damage it causes. My story is a bit different. While my father wasn't there, that wasn't the main issue. My biggest issues stemmed from my relationship with my mother.

My mother was a very mean woman who would often beat me. I didn't have time to think about how bad a father I had, because I was so focused on how awful my mom was. She was a very bitter person, and there was a serious emptiness in my life because of her. So I blamed all of my issues on her. I also held the men in my life responsible for giving me the love she never gave me.

I'm happy to say that my relationship with my mother is much better now. Still, it was one of the reasons I decided to have sex. The truth is I always viewed sex as something I would only do when I got married. But I didn't want guys to leave me for women who were willing to have sex with them. So I gave in.

My first time was at the age of nineteen. I had tried to have intercourse twice in junior high, when I was sixteen, but it never worked out. The act was too physically painful to me; I would just cry which made guys want to stop.

During my high school years, someone told me you could get pregnant on your first try. So I told my partner I was pregnant, just to see what he would say. He said we both had a future and we were both in school, so I should get rid of the baby. That hurt me so badly that I did not want to have sex again until I got married. In any case, I didn't go "all the way" until I had graduated high school.

I believed that first guy (the one I lost my virginity to) was "the one." I loved him so much and believed we were going to get married. We were already having oral sex at the time. We tried intercourse a couple of times, but it hurt too much and he had to stop.

The point is that I wanted to have sex with him because I loved him. But I knew we weren't married, and I knew we should wait. Then one day I told God, "We are going to get married in the Spirit so we can have sex." In my mind, being married "in the Spirit" was sort of like salvation. Obviously, I was young and immature. I believed this guy would be "the one," no matter what. In my mind, I had to be with him.

For me, sex was a bond, a covenant between two people. As far as I was concerned, we didn't need a ceremony with a lot of people; we could come into covenant on our own, like people do with salvation. In this "spiritual marriage," I bonded with him and felt that I had to stick with him through thick and thin, weakness and health, as though we were officially married.

It was easy for me to settle for less than the best in our relationship. I would say, "I love him anyway," because I had given myself to him. With that, I believed I had to stay with him.

The relationship was on and off and lasted for a while, but not forever. It ended once we decided to move to Atlanta, partly because I felt that I wasn't good at sex. If I wasn't good at it, I didn't want it anymore. So I left the relationship.

After that I became sexually frustrated. I didn't know that I was supposed to enjoy sex until someone told me so. For me, sex had been more of a chore. It made me cry so much that my ex used to stroke me and then go to sleep. I never told him the truth—that sex was unfulfilling to me.

After moving to Atlanta, I wanted to see whether I was the problem, so I decided to try sex again, this time with a guy I knew from back home. He wasn't as "well endowed" as my previous partner, so instead of being painful, the sex we had was enjoyable and fulfilling. I felt like more of a player, so to speak.

Even though I was having sex, I didn't give it up to just anyone. I sought out guys with "taste," guys who liked popular "high-end" girls. If the guy was popular that was even better, because he was more valuable to me. I wasn't running around with a lot of guys, so my reputation was still considered good. No one knew what I was up to, because I did it undercover.

During the transition away from the guy I loved, I dated another guy. I wanted to fill the void I felt from the breakup. In my mind I was also making up for all those times I wanted to have intercourse, but couldn't.

When I tried having sex with this guy, it didn't work. I believe that something in my spirit told me he wasn't worthy. Really, there were other issues for me; in the back of my head I thought sex was dirty.

First Thessalonians 4:3 says: "This is the will of God, your sanctification: that you should abstain from sexual immorality…." I guess, deep down, I knew it. Suddenly, trying to have sex with this guy felt more like I was being raped. He saw the look on my face and stopped. He said he just couldn't do it. He came back another day, and even a third time, but it did not work out.

Finally, I gave myself a talking to: "You have to do this. If you don't, you are going to lose him!" But I still couldn't do it, and I told him so. He said it was OK, and we could just kiss. I agreed to that, when all of a sudden, he just did it; he penetrated me with no warning and no protection. It was the scare of my life. After that, I knew I had to get my life together.

I answered the altar call for salvation and rededication, but continued going to the club and searching for that one right guy. One guy I already knew came to see me in January 2012. I reasoned to myself that it was OK to have sex with him because we'd had relations in the past.

But after him, that was it. I didn't have sex again. I pleasured myself at times, but got serious about celibacy in March of 2012. God started surrounding me with people who shared my views and helped me grow up as a person. Nobody was telling me what to do; I just listened to people's stories. What they shared gave me the push I needed to want to do better and to become celibate.

To me, celibacy means waiting till the right time to share intercourse with that special, right person. The walk of celibacy hasn't been hard yet because there is no special person in my life. I'm not dating and I'm not interested in anyone. I have challenges with masturbation, however. Over the past couple of weeks, I have had two dreams about it. In the dreams I told myself, "No, because God would not be pleased."

I think God has definitely helped me. This year the same guy came back to visit. We even slept in the same bed, and didn't do anything. (I don't recommend everyone trying that, by the way!) I told him that I wasn't doing anything with him and I stuck to it.

Right now, I feel that this is a new walk and I don't want to like anyone. That being said, I would enjoy kissing someone. I believe I can kiss without taking it to the extreme. We'll see whether I'm right about that.

Boundaries

Because I have just started the celibacy journey, I don't have a long list of boundaries yet. For now, I feel as though anything besides touching and intercourse are OK. I believe I can handle anything, but that's only because I have no interests at the moment. If I were interested in someone, these would be my boundaries:

- No contact with or between body parts.

- No playful sexual antics.

- No sexual talk.

Because I'm not having sex, kissing would be intense. I read an article that says you shouldn't kiss while dating because it can cause arousal. I can only speak for myself, but for me, getting aroused wasn't easy. It would take an hour of very intimate foreplay before I was "ready."

At least that was true before I started watching pornography. Then I was aroused very easily. It got to where I watched porn when masturbating, as though, if I could hurry up and finish, God wouldn't find out. Really, I knew it was wrong, and God started to convict me on it and I stopped.

Scripture says it all:

> *For this you know, that no fornicator, unclean person, nor covetous man, who is an idolater, has any inheritance in the kingdom of Christ and God* (Ephesians 5:5).

For now, the three boundaries I listed are all that I have. As long as my interaction doesn't bring up lustful thoughts, then I feel as though I should be OK. I know my thought-life is important. The Bible says we should be "casting down arguments and every high thing that exalts itself against the knowledge of God, bringing every thought into captivity to the obedience of Christ…" (2 Cor. 10:5; see also Ps. 19:14).

Sometimes you can't control which thoughts come to mind, but you can choose to think about something else. Because I really want to do this (celibacy) for God, whatever sex drive I had seems to be turned off.

I honestly feel like I can sleep with a guy in the same bed and not get caught up in the wrong desires. (Again, I can only speak for myself.)

God is my strength and I'm handling things well. I had a guy come over till about 2:30 in the morning. We sat on opposite sides of the sofa and nothing happened. I know he didn't come over with any motives, so there weren't any desires there.

So far, I haven't been convicted of having guys sleep over because nothing happens. I like to cuddle and just have company. One of my guy friends from back home wants to come see me. I know he is not going to look for a place to stay because, in his mind, he is going to stay with me. I don't see the point in having him find someplace else. I could be wrong, but I'm confident nothing is going to happen. I did kiss this guy when I was back at home, so I guess we will see how it goes when I see him.

Advice

Celibacy saves us from a lot of destruction and unhealthy emotional ties. If you're not celibate, by the time you get with your husband, it's not worth it anymore. Hebrews 13:4 talks about the marriage bed being undefiled. I think that's why I originally felt so strongly about holding on to my virginity.

If you have sex continually before marriage, you won't have anything to look forward to when you get married. Sexual intimacy wouldn't add that special spice to your relationship. Sex really is a gift to be unwrapped when you say "I do."

Deciding to become celibate is not only an instruction from God. Everything God tells us to do is for our own good. Celibacy prevents us from being in emotional distress and a lot of unnecessary drama. Sex makes up relationships and breaks them up, too. Everything today is based on sex. If you're celibate, you have more control over your life.

It may be that women don't wait until marriage because society doesn't see waiting as being normal anymore. It's so weird! People used to make fun of me when I was seventeen and still a virgin. They acted like I was dumb or slow. They would laugh at my boyfriend because it was obvious that I hadn't had sex with him. They would use sex lingo, and I never knew what they were talking about.

I feel that people don't want to wait because they are too worried about not being in the "in crowd." They want to be seen as being "normal." Being a virgin seems the same to them as having no sex appeal.

Guys I know said they didn't want virgin girlfriends; they preferred someone with more experience. Even today, guys say a girl brings more to the table if she's wearing a bikini in her social media profile pictures.

I disagree! I believe her character should speak the loudest in a photo. A female took issue with me on that. She said, "You should chill out. It's only Twitter." But social media should never be an excuse to fade down your character. Your character is not something to be turned on and off.

It's attractive to be a virgin and wait till marriage! I think some people fear not being "good enough" in the bedroom, so instead of waiting till marriage to have sex, they "practice" while they're single.

It's understandable that women who don't have a spiritual connection with God reason this way. Nowadays, it is difficult to find a good guy who will come around and not expect sex. There are a lot of horrible guys out there. Women get used to it and start thinking that's the best they can do.

Personally, I think women are going to the wrong places to meet guys. If we are not going to church and seeking God, we will never believe that He can find us that special guy. Special guys aren't at the clubs!

That's where I used to go thinking it was the easiest way to meet someone. I went to socialize and have fun. Then I'd have one sexy dance with a guy and think, "Maybe he's 'the one.'"

When we have sex with guys (outside marriage), they eventually get bored and leave anyway. The problem is we're accustomed to settling for the wrong guys in the wrong places.

Things get even harder when your boyfriend leaves you for another girl. The first thought is that he left because she was better in bed. I know I used to think that when I wasn't sexually active. Then when I got involved, but couldn't do all the stuff everyone else was doing, I felt like the guy would leave me if I didn't get my skills up. One ex-boyfriend definitely made me feel that way.

Sex was always something for them, not for me. They needed the sex, but I needed my emotional needs filled. That's why I kept them around. Now I have God's Joy. He meets my emotional needs!

If you're a woman who wants to be celibate, I would suggest that you don't stop everything at once. For example, if I decided to diet, I wouldn't go completely vegetarian tomorrow. I would start gradually introducing vegetables into my diet.

Some experts would disagree, but I believe you just have to start somewhere. Give up something, and go from there. If you are already on the celibacy journey and want to stay on track, I would suggest not being so vulnerable to guys that you'll compromise just to keep them.

You can be sexy without disrespecting God. Lustful thoughts will be less of a problem if you are focused on God and hanging with the right group of people.

If lustful thoughts are giving you trouble, it's because you are doing something you shouldn't be doing. Maybe you are hanging out with the wrong people or seeking the wrong things. If you are enjoying an intimate relationship with God, celibacy won't be difficult. When you are genuinely seeking Him, there shouldn't be any battles. Just follow His instructions, because the instructions you follow determine the future you create.

Abbey's "No Sex, What's Next?" Checklist

- Don't have sex to keep a man.

- Know who you are in God.

- Stay away from lustful thoughts.

- If you are a virgin, continue on that path. It's so attractive!

- Stay away from the "in crowd." It's much better to take the road less traveled (celibacy).

- Start the journey one step at a time.

- Know yourself to know your boundaries.

- Treat sex as gift to be opened after you say "I do."

- Get spiritually connected to God.

Message from God

My child, you are lost. But I will help you find your way. If you walk with Me, you will realize that My yoke is easy and My burden is light. Come to Me for comfort for I am your Father. I know the plans that I have for you, plans to prosper you. I'm working on you. Allow Me time to work on your behalf. My child, if you knew what I have planned for you, then you would understand. The plans that I have for you are vast, like how far the east is from the west. Await My plans for your life.

Allow God to Fight the Battle for You

Chapter 3

Na'imah:
Masturbating in
Elementary School
It Felt Good, So Why Not?

"Foods for the stomach and the stomach for foods, but God will destroy both it and them. Now the body is not for sexual immorality but for the Lord, and the Lord for the body" (1 Corinthians 6:13).

My Story

I'm Na'imah. I'm twenty-five years old and have been celibate for one year. My mindset has always been: "I'm not the kind of chick who's stuck on stupid for a guy she barely knows—I don't care how 'in love' she thinks she is."

When it came to sex, I always thought: "Let me get past the hurting part and on to the 'feeling good' part of it." I knew some scriptures; I even stood on some to keep me pure. But there came a time in my life when I just wanted to "do me." Unfortunately, I was only fifteen, and I didn't have the PEACE to know that God would take care of everything.

I can link my decisions around sex to my father not being around. I had a stepdad, in a sense, but he and my mom weren't married. It was a weird scenario; we never spoke to each other. He was around, but it wasn't a real relationship between people who actually communicate. Still, I had respect for him, even in the midst of the weirdness.

My father wasn't around at all, so I never got affirmation from him. I didn't hear him say that I was beautiful or that I was anything else good, so I looked for that attention from guys.

The kind of attention I sought had its own problems. I can remember people telling me that sex would hurt the first time, but the more you did it, the better it would feel. Because I didn't want to be the "I fell head over heels in love with him" type of chick, I decided that my first time would be with a guy I was dating.

Because of his small build, I thought there was a good chance the sex would not be painful. I was in for a rude awakening. The first time hurt a lot. Yet it only increased my determination to reach the point where it felt good.

What I wanted was a physical feeling, not necessarily the emotions or attachment. So I didn't sleep with every Tom, Dick, or Harry that came along. I was selective about who I slept with. I usually chose friends or people I had known for a while.

None of my friends told me not to do life this way because, for months, I didn't tell anyone I was having sex. If I had, someone would have spoken up, because from the sixth to the tenth grade a bunch of us took vows of purity at our church.

We attended meetings where people talked about purity, STDs, and teenage motherhood. We were made aware of all the reasons not to have sex before marriage. Then, at the end of the event, we took our vows and put on jewelry our parents gave us to signify the promise. Those who knew they weren't going to keep their vows just mumbled something under their breath—but it wasn't the words of the vow.

Around that time, I lost my virginity. Even though I knew better, I made a conscious decision to have sex. As I think back on my experiences and the decisions I made, all I can do is shake my head. Now I sit and read First Corinthians 6:15-16 and realize what it all means:

> *Do you not know that your bodies are members of Christ? Shall I then take the members of Christ and make them members of a harlot? Certainly not! Or do you not know that he who is joined to a harlot is one body with her? For "the two" He says, "shall become one flesh."*

I can say that my members were "members of a harlot." I was doing things that the members of Christ's Body should not be doing. I became "one flesh" with many men, not realizing what it would take to undo those spiritual ties.

As I think about it now, my dealings with sex started when I was in preschool. A little girl touched me inappropriately. I knew it wasn't right, and I wondered, "Where did she get that from?"

When I got to kindergarten, I began watching porn. Once my mom went to sleep, I would sneak out of my room to watch it. I didn't really know what it was, but it became normal to me.

This went on for years and years. It was more of an addiction to the idea of sex than to sex itself. Whether I was in church, at school taking an exam, or even praying, I could not go a single minute without thinking about sex. Not until recently did I realize this was a problem.

Preschool and kindergarten were just the foolery that prepared me for more. By the time I was in elementary school, I was masturbating regularly. My thought was that it felt good, so why not do it? Then, by the time I engaged in sex, I was desensitized to it, because I had watched it so many times on television.

Thinking back to those early years, I didn't know exactly what I was doing; but I knew I wasn't supposed to do it in front of people. It was ridiculous—I masturbated every day. That old "if it feels good, why not?" mentality stayed with me until about a year ago.

Eventually, when I had a boyfriend, I would masturbate and then have sex with him. (Masturbation was part of my life, like a part-time job, really.) Having sex and switching partners was not uncommon for me. In fact, it would be a long time before I developed the mindset that lust wasn't normal. It was years before I understood that, with discipline and commitment, the unholy ties established through sex could be broken.

Before I committed to celibacy, I used guys as tools. They were objects to me. There wasn't a guy out there who had my heart. Even the guy I lost my virginity to could not keep me; I had sex with him two or three times, and got bored because he didn't satisfy me. For the next month and a half, I found another partner. After three or four months, I moved on again. After that, I decided to be celibate for a while. Then I went back to pleasuring myself. I did whatever I wanted to do, although I remained mindful of the partners I chose.

I lived with a man for a year and a half. We said that we loved each other but I knew I didn't really mean it. What I liked was what he brought to the table, which was sex. Guys were my way to get attention and sex. No one ever won my real emotions or my heart. The relationships typically ended when I got tired of them, and wanted something different.

Even in my last relationship, we weren't really together. He was more like a friend to me—with the added benefit of sex. Eventually, I had to cut off the relationship. I couldn't keep living for God and doing that stuff anymore.

Second Corinthians 5:21 says that "He made Him who knew no sin to be sin for us, that we might become the righteousness of God in Him." I decided to start the journey to celibacy. There were a couple more slip-ups; then I got serious about it.

God knew what I had been doing. I knew He was not pleased, and I could not continue that way. The Bible says: "We must all appear before the judgment seat of Christ, that each one may receive the things done in the body…whether good or bad" (2 Cor. 5:10).

I felt that celibacy was about my keeping to myself completely—no touching, no feeling, no nothing. My mind had to be celibate as well as my body. This journey would be different from abstinence. Abstinence is more about staying away from something for a period of time. Celibacy is about starting something new and continuing in it.

For me, I needed to find that place of purity, because with purity you reach a whole new level. You can be celibate and still be thinking about having sex. You can also be celibate without being a born-again believer.

Purity and holiness were what I needed; they go hand in hand. When you are pure, you are keeping yourself for a greater reason. Purity is singleness in life; you are complete and whole just as you are. You don't need anything else but God.

Right now, I'm in a weird place on this celibacy journey. I'm trying not to make everyone my husband. I need to trust the Lord and not do my own thing (see Prov. 3:5). Before, I would see a guy and ask myself, "Is he the one?"

Soon enough, I would tell myself, "You're not ready anyway. We have other things to do—but he could still be the one. We sure would have pretty babies."

At the moment, I'm not interacting with guys on the dating level, and haven't been on a single date this past year. For now, I just see guys as good friends. Any conversations I have with them can be had in front of everyone.

This journey hasn't been all that hard for me. When thoughts come up, I cut them off immediately. I want to keep my mind on the right things (see Rom. 12:2). It's easier now because I made the decision for myself.

That doesn't mean I did everything right. I was born again and speaking in tongues when I first started messing around with the last guy. The church that I attend had just started a twenty-one-day fast, and I slept with this guy on day one.

Yes. I was fasting and having sex! It happened because I hadn't been tempted for a while and didn't recognize my weaknesses. I thought, "It's been eight months and nothing has happened, so I'm good."

Then I saw this guy with a lot of muscles, and realized I might have spoken too soon. After six months of messing around, I realized that the situations I repeatedly put myself in were *not worth it*. I was so over the nonemotional sex thing. I had no real ties with any of those men. It was fun while it lasted, but I was left with nothing, and always found myself back where I started from.

The worst part was starting all over again. Yet it was the best decision I ever made, and the difficulty was worth it. A passage in the Book of James explains:

> *My brethren, count it all joy when you fall into various trials, knowing that the testing of your faith produces patience* (James 1:2-3).

One of my ex-boyfriends is still around, but because we grew up together we are more friends than anything. He is not born again, so that relationship is definitely not going anywhere. God has a lot of work to do with him.

As for everyone else, I have cut them off completely. I am an entirely different person from the one they knew. They don't want to talk about what I am talking about anyway. These days, all I want to discuss are the love, mercy, and grace of Jesus (see Eph. 2:1-8).

And I have His Peace.

Boundaries

For my part, I have no idea what boundaries to set. I had notions about dating curfews, but the more I pray about it, the more I'm able to let God work it out and work on me. He says I don't have to worry about boundaries because he will set them Himself. So, there is no longer a time restriction on my dates.

In case they might be helpful to others, I will offer some boundaries that have worked for me in the past:

- No touching me. I'm very conscience of guys touching my arms or tapping my shoulders, for example. That's too much for me. A little church hug with two taps on the back is enough.

- I can't watch anything on television. I refuse to let my mind wander because I know how dangerous that can be for me.

- Men are not allowed to go upstairs in my house. There was a time when they weren't allowed to come to the house at all. Now I feel it is OK, but only if they stay downstairs. The guy I'm currently dating may be allowed into the living room at some point. We'll see, but I'm not quite sure about that yet.

- I cannot let myself gaze at a man too long, because seeing his muscles, legs, and lips can get me into trouble. For me, I consider it a sin. Instead of looking, I need to bow my head and pray.

God is showing me that I'm not as vulnerable as I think I am. He has informed me that I can lower my guard just a little from the "high security" level I have maintained for some time. God has shown me that I have to drop my guard slightly or no one will be able to enter my world at all.

Advice

I believe society has distorted things. Women feel that the only way they can get guys is by having sex with them. So many women don't have fathers at home; as a result, they don't know their real self-worth. They end up believing that compromising to have a guy for a night or even a couple of hours is worth it.

We don't have to settle! We women can change the standard. We can change society. If we would just keep ourselves pure, we could accomplish great things!

We also need to watch what we are taking in. When I got really serious about celibacy, I knew that watching or listening to certain things was off limits. For example, I know better than to listen to rhythm and blues music (R & B), because it sets me off.

Here's some more advice: beware of the conversations you have with guys. Don't let them take the dialogue where you don't want it to go. The same is true for your thought life: don't dwell on sex, because whatever you continuously think about, you will eventually do, as James explained:

> *But each one is tempted when he is drawn away by his own desires*
> *and enticed. Then, when desire has conceived, it gives birth to sin;*
> *and sin, when it is full-grown, brings forth death* (James 1:14-15).

You have to be determined. After a year of watching my "intake," I can stop myself from looking at a guy the wrong way. Now I tell myself, "He may not be your husband, and with those thoughts, you are cheating on your husband."

I also want to share something with women who continually have sex: You may be doing this because you think you will never get married. But really, you are lost. Find out who you are, because living promiscuously and not wanting to be married are signs that you don't own yourself. You are renting out your body. Excuse me for saying this, but someone is pimping you.

That is no way to live. At some point you will want to settle down. You'll realize that all those people in your past have a piece of you, and you have nothing. I promise you, it will get old at some point, so please, value yourself more. Say what God's Word says about you: "…I am fearfully and wonderfully made… (Ps. 139:14).

That is the truth!

Na'imah's "No Sex, What's Next?" Checklist

- Do away with lust.
- Know your worth.
- Don't allow your past to dictate your future.
- View guys as more than just objects.
- Listen to God.
- Watch what you are taking in.
- Cut off wicked thoughts immediately.
- Get your affirmation from God.
- Seek to please God.

Message from God

My child, you are a blessing to behold. There are more things I want to teach you. Yes, you are listening to Me and adhering to My voice, but more work is yet to be done. Allow My words to penetrate your soul. Then you will allow them to take root and grow on the inside of you. Know that if you listen to Me, you can't go wrong. I am the Lord your God. I won't lead you astray. You might not understand right away, but trust Me. I have everything under control. If you give your life to Me, it will never be the same again. You won't go back to those others. You will push forward knowing that I have your life in My hands. That's the only place it needs to be. Don't try to take back control, because I can do a better work than you can. My ways are not your ways; My thoughts are not your thoughts. So just trust in Me and allow Me to guide you. All things will come to pass. Just trust in Me.

Allow God Into Your Life

Chapter 4

*C*ADEE:

IT AIN'T EASY...

BUT HIS GRACE IS SUFFICIENT

"And he said unto me, My grace is sufficient for thee: for my strength is made perfect in weakness. Most gladly therefore will I rather glory in my infirmities, that the power of Christ may rest upon me. Therefore, I take pleasure in infirmities, in reproaches, in necessities, in persecutions, in distresses for Christ's sake: for when I am weak, then am I strong" (2 Corinthians 12:9-10 KJV).

My Story

My name is Cadee. I'm thirty years old, and I've been celibate for ten years. It has been anything but easy. There were many times when I wanted to say, "You know what, God? This is for the birds. I had more fun when I was in the world."

Then I look back on all the hurt, pain, and disappointments that the affairs of the world brought to my life. Immediately, I "give thanks to the Lord, for He is good…His mercy endures forever" (Ps. 136:1).

Often, when the going was tough, I would read Colossians 1:11 and scratch my head. The verse talks about being "strengthened with all might, according to His glorious power, for all patience and *longsuffering with joy."*

My question was, "How do you operate in longsuffering with joy?" My journey in celibacy challenged me, but now I can say that I know what LONGSUFFERING "with joy" means.

Growing up, I was one of those kids who craved attention because I didn't have a father at home. I wasn't often told that I was beautiful. I did hear it, but only from my mother or other relatives—never from my father.

My biological father had some weird ideas. Other people would tell me the good things he said about me. He claimed he didn't tell them to me because he didn't want me to get a big head. I didn't understand the concept; what was the good of *not knowing* what my father felt about me?

Obviously, I'd never get a big head by not knowing, and I was never around my biological father to hear it anyway. I did have a stepfather. Nothing was ever good enough for him, so he wasn't handing out any compliments either. All in all, there was no father figure to help me know how I should expect guys to treat me.

I grew up in church all my life, and had ministers in my family. I knew scriptures, read scriptures, heard scriptures, and disregarded scriptures. I knew that I could always run to God if something went wrong, and I loved Him for it.

The problem was that I loved God for the blessings, healings, and other good things He could give me. I saw Him as some kind of magician. When I needed something, I would go to God. But I wasn't in love with Him. I didn't read my Bible regularly; I didn't do daily devotions. I knew how to be good according to the world's standard, but I didn't search out God's standards or what pleased Him.

Even with my knowledge of the Bible, I still wanted to have sex. Starting at the age of eighteen, I did. I don't think anything in particular triggered my first experience; I just knew I wanted to do it. It wasn't that I was deeply in love or anything like that. It was more that the guy was older and I felt comfortable with him. Having lots of sexual partners was something I wanted to avoid. But, because he was older and had "been around," I knew I could learn something from him.

Guys used to be a game to me. Being chased by them was fun. I fed off the attention, and liked the emotional buzz I got from keeping the rotation going and the calls coming in. The guys probably thought they were getting all the benefits, but I felt very much in control. As one guy rotated out, I rotated a new one in. It gave me a (false) sense of value to see how much they wanted me. I can remember coming home from college and listening to all the voicemail messages guys had left me. I got high just hearing them.

After my relationship with a certain guy ended, we kept playing house. I suddenly looked at myself and asked, "How did I get here? Why am I so far off course? This isn't where God wants me. Why am I clubbing, and drinking, and dealing with foolishness?"

I wondered how I'd come so close to doing what I swore I would never do, which was to repeat my mom's story. She never wanted that for me. I imagined different scenarios, like how hard it would be to tell her I was pregnant.

Then I wondered, "Why am I contemplating these things? How did I end up here? God has protected me so much. He positioned things in my life—so why am I still having sex with multiple partners?"

Finally, I took a step back and said, "This is not me." I was tired of the way I was living. I was *over it*. So I just broke down and said, "God, I need Your help. I'm done with this, and I'm drawing near to You the way Scripture says I should." (See James 4:8.)

I prayed a very rare but serious prayer: "God, You know my heart. You know I've been hurt in the past. You know I'm being broken down. I can't keep going through this. Please help me to bypass any relationships that are not from You. Don't let me take the wheel out of Your hands. I don't want any more unnecessary heartbreak or extra baggage."

After that prayer, I decided to become celibate. I was finished with the old life; I didn't want to live that way anymore. I wanted the new life Paul wrote about:

If anyone is in Christ, he is a new creation; old things have passed away; behold, all things have become new (2 Corinthians 5:17).

That's the life what I wanted, and celibacy was part of it. For me, celibacy means keeping my life pure before God. It means telling Him that my desire is to please Him rather than myself—not living outside of His will, but embracing whatever He has for me. Whatever journey He decides to take me on, I will do it in His pure and uncorrupted way, not mine.

I associated my journey with Psalms 18, which is foundational for me. It speaks of being cleansed and being held by God. It describes God as my shield, in whatever I must fight against. He is right there with me and can give me the grace to go through temptation. It doesn't even feel like a fight, because He's fighting for me (see Exod. 14:14). It is as though He's saying, "You stay with Me, and I will do the rest."

Now that I am walking with God, I don't see guys the same way anymore. I must admit, the whole reason I had sex the first time was because I was plotting—literally plotting against God. He said, "Don't do it," but I knew that if I did as I pleased, what was done would be done. He would not turn back the hands of time, but He would be faithful to forgive me (see 1 John 1:9).

Part of my scheming was to learn something about sex before my wedding night. So I took unholy advantage of God's forgiveness, and did things my way.

Now He has placed me on a path of purity. For me, this purity is His complete process of returning me to His original plan for my life. The plan was for me to be pure, to walk with Him, and to be presented without blemish, tainting, or corruption—and without the world imbedded in me.

I see things differently now. What I cared about before is not what I care about now. It's not about who I can get. Now, I want God's purpose; I want a divine connection. I recognize the negative effects of the situations I created and the drama those situations brought. It wasn't right, and I knew it. The pain associated with it was great; I don't want it anymore.

There are generational curses in my family, but I am working to keep them from going forward. So I let God take the wheel. Now, when I look at a guy, I assess his qualities beyond the physical ones. I look at his character; I try to understand what makes him who he is.

Before my commitment to celibacy, I looked for character, but the balance was way off. It was more a question of what a guy could do for me. Now it's a question of who he is, what he knows, and what his priorities are. If those aren't in line, we don't have much to talk about long-term.

I need to know if he is on the same page as I am. Is he trying to get something from me, or does he desire to live his life together with me? There is a big difference between the two!

Not only do I look at guys differently, but I also look at my pre-celibacy activities differently. For the first couple of years on my celibacy walk, I didn't realize masturbation was out. I thought God's order was, "No men."

I felt as though I was doing God's will, and it was awesome—the best of both worlds (or so I thought). I had my erotic books and the paraphernalia I used to get me to "the right place." I ran from any conversations about masturbation being wrong.

Eventually, I had to acknowledge the truth. It was a big deal getting rid of my "stuff." I felt like I was really alone at that point; and I was about to walk this thing out all by myself.

It wasn't easy to quit the erotica, because my flesh would rise up at times. My body was used to the wrong things; I had to go through a kind of detoxification, as if I were withdrawing from a substance. My body had forgotten how to live without sin. I wondered how I would ever get through it. I failed multiple times, and it hurt me afterward. But grace found its way to me.

What helped me to extend the spans of time between failures was the fact that I didn't want to start over. I knew God had promises for me and I did not want to fail Him anymore. I had to get to a place of being sorry for what I did—not just for having the sex but for intentionally plotting against Him.

Within the past year or two, I have become sorry about the plotting. Before that, I was only sorry about having to start again. It was all about me. But now, I'm sorry for displeasing God, and I know I'm moving forward with Him. "[I'm pressing] toward the goal for the prize of the upward call of God in Christ Jesus" (Phil. 3:14; see also, verses 12-13).

Boundaries

Everything I thought I would love to do with my own place, I can't do now. So, I have set some boundaries to keep me on track:

- My boyfriend can't stay over. We can't just cuddle up, chilling alone in my house on a regular basis. Doing this starts to feel too much like *our* home and *our* union.

- We can't talk about sex, not even on the phone, because it turns into phone sex.

- No massages. They are the trick of the enemy.

As our relationship continues, these boundaries may need to be better defined. For example, if my boyfriend were to stop me from initiating sexual advances—meaning he's leading the sexual purity—it would actually turn me on. It would intrigue me and lead me into "honoring" him more. I need to be careful!

There are some more specific things I need stay away from:

- The wrong scenes are off limits. I stay away from clubs and from drinking; I don't get around the same people I used to hang out with.

- I am very aware of what I watch on television. Sometimes I have to turn off the television altogether.

- I can't listen to certain music, and certain recording artists, because of the way they can affect me.

Celibacy is not all about what *not* to do. It also matters what you do when you feel a little crazy. When I am in a certain mood, I know I need to be in the Word. I can't say, "I will just miss church today." It is too easy to fall back, get comfortable, and let my flesh rise up. I know I don't want to go back where I came from, especially not when God keeps saying, "I'm preparing you for something, so don't mess up."

There are times when I want sex. That's when I try to stay distracted. That's a huge thing for me. I have to do something or go somewhere, to get in the Word or run an errand. I also have to lock my computer so that I can't get to certain sites. Yes, I have broken that rule, but I think it's inside me more now, because I'm so tired of failing.

My honesty in prayer has helped a lot. God has decreased my urges significantly over time. My mind still goes places. If I see a muscular guy, it brings up memories of old experiences. My flesh wants to go there, but I have to change my thoughts. He is faithful; He helps me to resist the temptation (see 1 Cor. 10:13). Temptations will come, but when they come, I can change my mind.

If you deal with thoughts like I do, just keep saying aloud, "This thing can't stay. It has to go!"

Advice

I believe women don't wait to have sex anymore because casual sex is the norm. For me, it was my fix. Whatever emotions were going on inside—whether I was happy, sad, mad, or frustrated—sex seemed like the perfect answer.

Sex is everywhere you turn: from media, to music, to movies. So many people are doing it because it's glorified everywhere. It seems as if women are thinking, "If I don't have sex, there is something wrong with me." So they engage in sex without understanding the depth and the impact of it.

There is much more to sex than what we see on television. We like to think there are no strings attached, but it's not so. There will always be some emotional attachment and the damage it causes. Sex always creates emotional issues.

There are also spiritual ties from sex. During sex, you are depositing and receiving harmful seeds. That is not God's will for you. He has something much better in mind. The longer your sex life is out of order, the longer you will remain disconnected from God's best and exposed to STDs, pregnancy, and a broken family life. It all starts with out-of-order sex.

Sex isn't a toy or a tool. It actually has a purpose that is reserved for a husband and wife (see Gen. 2:24). So women, understand your worth. I definitely didn't understand mine, and it cost me.

Most women don't see that their bodies are the temple of the Holy Spirit (see 1 Cor. 6:19-20). God definitely has a plan for you. In Jeremiah 29:11, God said: "I know the thoughts that I think toward you…thoughts of peace and not of evil, to give you a future and a hope."

Don't get caught up in sex. It's a trap from the enemy. It exposes you to unwanted outcomes. When you give in, you are letting down your guard and inviting all kinds of spirits to come into your physical, emotional, spiritual, and mental self. All these things can be manifested because of sex.

Celibacy is really a safeguard and a shield that keeps these spirits from gaining entry. If you take your shield down, the damage you suffer is self-inflicted. How sad it is to do such damage to yourself!

You don't have to. Just continue to walk and seek God. I know it might sound cliché, but as you continue with Him, He will bring you to new levels. He knows your heart and He knows when you are trying.

Because of Christ, there is no condemnation or expression of strong disapproval (see Rom. 8:1). God loves you. Please know that He freely offers all the attention you seek, at a deeper and more meaningful level than any human being can offer. But God needs all of you. Give Him all of you, and He will take you where He wants you to go.

Remember that purity is a process. It wasn't an immediate change in me, but God knew my heart. When I first said I wasn't going back to my old life, I knew guys were only a phone call away and I tried three times to set up something. God knew my weaknesses and shielded me. I was like a toddler who was trying to walk; when I was about to fall, my Father picked me up and kept me safe. He helped me though the toddler stages of my journey.

Always know this: He loves you deeply, and He will be there to take those baby steps with you.

Cadee's "No Sex, What's Next?" Checklist

- Know your worth.

- Remember that celibacy is a process.

- Understand that sex should not be used as a temporary fix.

- Seek God. He will then give you clear direction on your path.

- Understand that sex has a purpose, and that purpose is for a husband and a wife.

- Understand that once you are complete in God, He will take care of everything else.

- Seek attention from God, not man.

- Stay away from the wrong scenes.

- Renew your mind, both day and night.

Message from God

My child, you are great. Oh, My daughter, how I love you so much. Nothing you are doing makes Me disappointed in you. You might not think this is so, but it is. My child, know that I love you dearly. You are My child and, just as parents correct their children when needed, I will correct you. Right now, it's not needed. You make Me well pleased. You are this Father's delight. You, My child, are My treasure, more precious than diamonds. You are a creation of My glory. Others can see that glory on you. You carry My name and you are worthy of My love. Know that we walk hand in hand. There is nothing you will ever go through without Me. Mistakes will happen; that's why I am with you. There are great things to come, so just be patient. Know that you make Me smile every day. My heart and your heart beat as one. My child, you are a great treasure.

Don't Run Away From God

Chapter 5

$\mathcal{T}$ALICIA:

I DID STUPID THINGS...

BUT HE LOVED ME ANYWAY

"Therefore, [there is] now no condemnation (no adjudging guilty of wrong) for those who are in Christ Jesus, who live [and] walk not after the dictates of the flesh, but after the dictates of the Spirit" (Romans 8:1 AMP).

My Story

Many of the decisions I made in my past were knee-jerk reactions to things other people did to me. I'm not saying these reactions were right; but because I didn't show KINDNESS to myself, I used my body to get back at these people. If I had understood the rare value of what I possessed and who I was, I might have made very different choices.

I'm Talicia. I'm twenty-nine years old, and I've been celibate for seven months. I grew up in a two-parent household, which is rare in today's society. Although my father was present, it was almost like he wasn't.

Our parents wanted the best for us kids, so my father worked two or three jobs. His schedule made it impossible for him to attend certain school events. When he was home, I knew he loved me; but as a child I really didn't understand. I would say, "Daddy, you are always gone." I was upset and bitter about that for a quite a while.

Now that I am older, I understand what was going on. My father also realizes the effect his absence had on us. It bothers him, because he sees how close we are to our mother. Although we respect him, we are not close to him. We talk to our mother every day, but go weeks without talking to our father.

God has shown me that I need to make a conscious effort to talk to my father whenever I call home and speak to my mom. I don't want him to feel badly or think he did something wrong.

I know that a lot of women have issues with sex because their fathers weren't around. That's not my story. My issues were about me doing stupid things.

I consider myself a rare breed. First, I got into the whole sex game late. I was almost twenty-three when I first had sex. My views and my approach were always "outside the box." My boyfriend at the time questioned whether I was really a virgin. Because of my outside-the-box ideas about sex, he didn't believe I was a first-timer.

Even when I was having sex, I was not all over the streets like a whore. I had some upbringing and I was saved at the time; but I was also backsliding and out of fellowship. The truth is I loved sex and I loved to experiment. It was only His grace that kept me from giving myself away to every man who came along.

I know about being a "sex freak." It was part of my life. Without God, it still would be. When I see girls in church wearing little, short dresses, I don't judge them. The same is true of the prostitutes on the streets. I know how easy it would be to get to that point. That's why I thank God and tell Him, "great is Your mercy toward me…" (Ps. 86:13). If not for His mercy, I don't know where I would be.

Although I was selective about which men to have sex with, I gave them all of myself. I was very flirtatious and held nothing back. My thinking was that whatever I do, I have to be the best at it. If I know I can't sing, I won't try. I would want to be the best singer or not sing at all.

I wanted to be the best at sex, too. I wanted guys to say, "Talicia was better than my last girlfriend." If I hadn't pulled away, guys would still be calling me and reminiscing about the good ole days. One or two still creep back in and say, "You remember the good ole days…blah blah blah…." I let them know it's not happening like that anymore. But back in the day, it was, and it was all about me and sex.

My decision to have sex at age twenty-three was a bad one. I had waited all those years. Even when I was in college, men knew that I was smart, beautiful, and off limits sexually. My mind was made up; my husband would be the first man to touch me. I even prayed about it. I told God, "If I stumble and have sex, let that man be my future husband, so I can say my husband was my first. If we slip up, at least we can laugh about it later."

It didn't work out that way.

I remember my boyfriend during my college years; looking back I don't even know why I dated him. I had just moved to Syracuse, and he was still in South Carolina. We started butting heads because of the distance. Meanwhile, there was a guy in Syracuse who got my attention. It was like we really "clicked."

When I went home for Christmas and saw my boyfriend, things were different, and we had another big fight. He wanted to have sex and I didn't, so I returned to Syracuse. I kept calling him, but he wasn't calling back, which irritated me. So, I decided to hurt him with the one thing he wanted, which was sex. I told a friend of mine that I was going to go out and have sex with someone else.

I ended up going to a Halloween party with a guy I was dating on the side. I made up my mind: that would be the night. After a few drinks, it was a wrap. I lost my virginity. I didn't tell my boyfriend back home what I had done. At that point, I really didn't care.

That was the beginning of a cycle that continued throughout my time in Syracuse. As much fun as I was having, I knew it was wrong. I knew I was walking in "the way of the ungodly" (see Ps. 1:6).

God was still talking to me and dealing with me. Sometimes I wanted Him to leave me alone and let me get the sex I wanted. It's not like I didn't know the Scriptures. I would even tell guys, "This is wrong." Then, when the sex was done, I would repent.

God told me I wasn't really sorry, because I knew I was doing wrong and I kept doing it. Looking back, I wasn't trusting God to bring me all I wanted in a man. Instead, I tried to get it on my own. In the process, I connected with to the wrong people. I was trying to fill a void in my life by figuratively "marrying" myself to certain men. In my mind, what I was doing was OK because my level of commitment was high. Even though I didn't have a ring, in my heart, we were married.

I had talked myself into believing my story. Only now am I getting the revelation about the whole situation. God has told me, "All this happened because you didn't trust Me, and you didn't want to be a woman who saved herself until she was forty-five."

That was true; I knew women like that and it scared me. I wanted to live and enjoy my twenties. I didn't want to risk waiting until my body was old and unattractive. I wanted someone to see me in my youthful "glory."

My thoughts were carnal. The mind of my flesh had too much to say. (See Romans 8:6–8.) I knew better. Once I started in this lifestyle, I felt like I was abusing His grace and it was only a matter of time until it ran out.

There were times when I cried and prayed in dreaded fear as I took at-home pregnancy tests, hoping they weren't "positive." I knew I couldn't dodge that bullet forever; eventually I would have to call home and say I was pregnant. His grace sustained me. Thank God, I never had to make that phone call.

Still, God dealt with me. It got to a point where He said, "You want to be married, and I have given you what you need to be a great wife and a great mother. Why are you giving it to someone who was not created for you?"

God's Word says that He creates a man's helper (see Gen. 2:18). So, when He spoke to me, it hit me hard. I said, "OK, God. You have some-one for me and You are going to bring him to me. But because I haven't waited, I'm cheating on the person You created for me."

That's when purity started to make sense, and I decided to become celibate. I won't pretend that it's easy, because it's not. But I can do this because the payoff is worth it. His Word says, "Be holy, for I am holy" (1 Pet. 1:16). There isn't much more to say.

Several times before making my commitment, I had tried what I thought was celibacy. I guess it was more like abstinence, really. I did a round of abstaining at the age of twenty-five, but it didn't last. When I was twenty-six, I got serious again; but again I slipped up.

The devil knows what makes us tick. Scripture says that he "walks about like a roaring lion, seeking whom he may devour" (1 Pet. 5:8). At the same time, I think a lot of my choices were knee-jerk reactions to something else.

For example, this one guy was my closest friend. After almost a year, I felt like we should have been more than friends. He said things that hinted at a future, but I was thinking, "You need to hurry up and make a decision."

When he entered basic training, I lost my patience. I was disappointed that he didn't stay back home with me, so I turned the tables on him and had sex with someone else. I should have waited on God to work out our relationship; but I took things into my own hands and messed them up.

That kind of behavior was common for me. Since then, I have recognized that pattern and stopped it. I no longer react to situations out of pure emotion.

Instead, I take my celibacy walk very seriously. To me, it is a cleanup process. God is undoing something that I shouldn't have done in the first place. It's my second chance to get it right. It's also a matter of understanding, accepting, and being faithful to the idea that sex was made for a husband and wife.

Celibacy is part of the process of preparing and reprogramming for the ultimate goal of marriage. It is a lifestyle that takes a conscious effort to achieve. It starts with your thinking. It means putting the old life behind, renewing the mind, and walking in the new nature (see Eph. 4:22-24). Once you decide to become celibate, you open the door for purity. Once you realize that you are pure, you set your standards higher and place more value in yourself.

Back in the old days, things "just happened" for me. Now certain choices are deal-breakers. I no longer want to catch a man's eye for the wrong reasons, because I know I bring value and worth to the table. I don't want to be a vixen anymore. Things that used to be acceptable are no longer acceptable. My interaction with men has changed because I see myself as more than just an object. It's going to take more for a man to be with me. The purer my mindset, the more my thought process changes, and the less likely I am to fall for the wrong people and situations.

Now that I'm able to sift out people's motives, I'm a little more selective about guys. I avoid certain situations; I know that if I play with fire, it's a matter of time before I get burned. If I don't feel that a person's motives are totally pure, I won't deal with that person. It's hard enough battling with myself! I have had to cut off a lot of people, because even if they did mean well, I might become tempted. With certain people, I'm just too vulnerable. Thoughts and images from the past would come into play.

I'm very straightforward about everything now. I don't want anyone to think they are dating me. I'm not giving them a chance to believe that, after a "reasonable amount of time" has passed, they can cash in. No, sir. Depending upon who I think you are, it may or may not come up on the first date—but by the second date you will know that I am not having sex with you.

I don't want to feel like I'm misrepresenting myself to anyone. I love myself so much right now, and I know that I have much to offer. My whole mindset about purity and modesty has changed. I used to be so proud of my physical assets that I showed them off for the world to see. I no longer want to be the type of person who advertises one thing and says another. If I tell you I'm celibate, I want my appearance to say it. I'll only "advertise" what I'm actually "selling."

Boundaries

To establish the right boundaries, you have to know yourself and the person you are interacting with. Boundaries can change depending on who is involved. Here are some of my boundaries:

- Not just anyone can come to my house for a movie night. Only one of my friends comes over (and vice versa), because we have the same boundaries. The bottom line is that you really have to know the person.

- I don't want anyone calling me after a certain hour. Calling me after midnight is especially dangerous. Guys think my bedroom voice is sweet and then they want to come over. So I tell them, "Don't call me late at night."

- First dates are scheduled for daytime hours, when I feel less vulnerable to loneliness and less likely to want to cuddle. It gives me time to get to know the person and figure out how much of a wall I have to put up. It is also easier for like-minded people to deal with boundaries in the daytime.

- I avoid being too playful. I am careful not to kiss in certain ways that set guys off.

When you are celibate, you place more value on kissing and hugging. You'll find that when you are not giving in to sex, even a full embrace can affect you. Instead, a modest church hug will keep things straight. Even holding someone's hand means more when you know that sex is out of the question.

Advice

Be mindful of your actions. Anything that invites fornication or an opportunity for fornication is sin. Temptation is dangerous and often leads to sinful acts (see James 1:14-15).

I don't believe kissing is wrong, but I believe that if my intent is to get a man turned on, it's a sin, because I have ignited turmoil within him. If you do something that causes your brother to fall, then you have sinned as well. I don't want to cause that type of offense for anyone.

As far as dressing modestly, the Bible doesn't specifically say what not to wear. The issue is intent; if you choose outfits that you know will stimulate men, then it's wrong. Playing with fire is testing God (see Matt. 4:7).

At one point I thought having oral sex was not sinning. I tried to justify myself. I told God that if I gave up intercourse, I should be able to have *some* pleasure. He didn't buy my rationale. Instead, He brought conviction.

That is what I needed—to learn that God is very good at convicting us. When things aren't right, He says so. He knows what our individual issues are. For some of my friends, sleeping in the same bed with someone is not temptation. I'm not so sure that could work for me. I would probably want to be held, and who knows where that might lead. You have to know yourself. Just because your friend can handle something doesn't mean you can handle it.

Kissing is an issue for me. If I take it too far, then I'm gone. Once I'm over that edge, it's too late. I'm not thinking anymore and I can't shut it off. Even if I hear God talking to me, I would be liable to say, "I hear You, but it's too late to talk to me. I've already messed up. It's over."

Knowing my limits is important. Some people can watch certain things on television that I cannot watch. I'm very sappy and romantic, so watching a soap opera is trouble. I'll start having dreams and fantasies and eventually find a way to make them happen.

Like I said, you really do have to know yourself. We women are emotional. We want to be held and loved. Some people think that once you get saved all that goes away, but it doesn't. We are still women and that is how we are built. We have these desires inside us; that's where the struggle comes in.

We have to speak to ourselves. We have to say, "Flesh, stay in your place and know your role. I am a spirit being, above all."

When your Boaz comes along and marries you, you can have all the sex you want. Until then, you need to calm down and hold your ground. I used to ask God whether I should pray for the sexual woman inside me to die. Then I thought about it and realized that I didn't really want her to die. She was created for a reason. Now my prayer is not that she dies, but that my spirit overcomes and keeps her in check.

God places certain qualities in us. There are women who were created to be mothers. It's just in them. Other women see marriage as a ministry; they see the benefit of two becoming one flesh. They don't want to get married for prestige or money.

When used properly, a women's sexuality is healthy. Some people in the church think that it's wrong and shouldn't be there; but it should be there, because we were created to be sexual beings. It's not wrong or nasty. It isn't some demon that needs to be prayed out of us. It's something that we just have to put in check until we're married.

Women, when times get hard, pray harder. I know there are times when I can't call and be around certain people. It's just biological. So I stay home alone and watch a movie. There are times when I don't want to even talk to certain people on the phone. I don't want to say anything that will get them going, because it will only turn into phone sex. On those days, I don't even touch my phone. When I'm going through these weak moments, it's just me and God.

Listen to the instructions God has set for you. I have listened, and then fallen back. I was told to cut off certain people, and I did. Then, somehow, they would call me and their numbers would be saved in my phone again. I have learned to clean that up. Most of the time talking to them wouldn't lead to anything serious. But I have to be watchful, especially since none of my relationships ended badly. At least if they had, we would never have talked again.

Over time, God has allowed me to understand why I tended to put myself in certain situations. Now, I know who I am, what makes me tick, and why I make certain decisions. I know what my ultimate goals are and what I want. I'm not walking blindly anymore. That has really helped me.

Too often, women don't know themselves. Therefore, they don't know how to deal with people and have healthy relationships. It's like trying on lots of pairs of shoes until you find the right fit. You can try on shoes all day long and never find the right match. Instead of trying on lots of men, just try God. He will bring the right fit for and to you.

Celibacy is one of the greatest life choices you could ever make for your future. Maybe you have never seen the "ultimate marriage" or witnessed anyone you know getting married. That doesn't mean marriage isn't in your future. But it needs to be God's way. He has specific guidelines as to what a family unit looks like.

God talks about a man and woman coming together to be fruitful and have dominion over the earth (see Gen. 1:27-28). He has given us clear instructions; it only makes sense that He knows how to make the pieces fall together. He will have the right people find each other. He will teach them how to be happy and operate as a unit.

Not everyone has grown up around positive images of marriage. All they see are alarming divorce rates, generations without fathers and grandfathers, and grandmothers acting as heads of the family. I can understand how this would paint marriage in a bad light. Yet when you see that marriage is what God desires and has ordained, you can operate in faith, "the substance of things hoped for" (Heb. 11:1), and you will have it. Marriage is in God's Word; He "is not a man, that he should lie" (Num. 23:19).

Come to Him with a heart that's right and pure. Say to God, "I don't think this marriage thing can happen, but Your Word says that this is what You want for Your people. You say that I can't have sex until marriage, and that marriage is a reward. So be it. I will trust You, Lord. I believe You can make it happen."

Talicia's "No Sex, What's Next?" Checklist

- When times get rough, pray harder.

- Have your inner vixen submit to your spirit.

- See celibacy as a cleanup and reprogramming stage in your life.

- Place more value in yourself.

- Cut off old relationships.

- Be selective. Not everyone is worthy of your time.

- Allow God to start a work in you from the inside out.

- Don't react solely on emotions. Think before you act.

- Know the people you are dealing with and stick to your boundaries.

Message from God

Ha ha, My child. You make Me laugh. The way you see the world brings joy to My face. You see it in a way that most don't. You will be that light that people will look to in order to ease their way. Continue to walk in Me. Continue to show people My way with your personality and smile. Those are talents that I have given you to bring people back to Me. Leave your past right where it is and don't pick it up again. We have much to do in the future, and your past won't be needed. I am training you to be the best. I know that you will be with Me. You are My child; you are not to be mistaken for anyone else. My daughter…My glory…My headstrong child—continue to follow Me and tell people your story. They will listen and follow your advice. They will be won over with your story because they need to hear it. Stay where you are and don't move until I tell you. I have some things in the works for you— great things. Just wait and see. The delight that you have been asking for is right around the corner. Just wait and see.

God Will Wait on You

Chapter 6

*U*HERI:
I FELT LIKE
I WASN'T WORTHY...

BUT GOD TOLD ME THAT I WAS

"I will praise You, for I am fearfully and wonderfully made' marvelous are Your works, and that my soul knows very well" (Psalms 139:14).

My Story

Hi, I'm Uheri. I have often felt like I wasn't worthy of being in a relationship because I have two children. But God told me that I am worthy. He explained that He has everything I need. He said His GOODNESS would supply all my needs—but I have to trust Him. Now I trust Him, and I live in expectation of seeing His will for my life.

I did not always trust God. I grew up in a two-parent household with a father so strict I didn't even think about having sex. In our house, avoiding pregnancy was the only real reason to abstain from sex. There was no biblical principle involved. We didn't even go to church. I got saved because someone knocked on my door and told me about Jesus Christ.

My mother always told me not to answer the door, but this time, I did. It wasn't a Jehovah Witness knocking, either. It was a woman from a Baptist church. I was nine years old at the time. The woman talked to me about who Jesus was, and I got saved that very day. She made arrangements for friends of hers to take me to church. When they couldn't, the church van picked me up. My parents were OK with my attending, but they didn't go with me.

I attended church until I was a teenager. I'm not sure why I stopped going or what the transition was. By the time I quit church, I had a good foundation. The children's ministry taught us kids to memorize lots of scriptures. Whenever I went through difficulty, I was able to draw on what was stored in my memory.

Always, I prayed, even throughout high school, when I was with my children's father. I used to pray and ask God, "Should I be with him? Lord, can You help me?" Even those long ago prayers are part of where I am today. The fact that my children's father and I are no longer together is an answer to prayer.

Now, I'm thirty years old. The first time I had sex was at the age of sixteen. I never talked to my parents about it, so no one knew. I didn't even mention having a boyfriend. I wasn't allowed to have one, so I kept it secret.

Eventually the truth came out. I wanted to go out more, and didn't want to do what I was should have been doing. My parents probably knew more than they let on; I don't think they wanted to talk about certain issues, so they didn't bring them up.

When I had sex, I did so because I knew it meant something. To me, you had to love someone to have sex with him. My children's father and I stayed together for several years. I was content to know we were together and loved each other. In my mind, sex naturally followed.

My two closest friends and I didn't talk about sex, so I had no idea whether they were doing it. One girl was Pentecostal. Her mom was so strict that she wasn't even allowed to look at a boy. My other friend always had boyfriends. I think she was sexually active, but she never mentioned it.

The only thing the three of us talked about was menstrual cycles. We were a more reserved group compared to the other girls at school. Our mentality was simple: we just wanted to find ourselves boyfriends. That was it. I had only one boyfriend in high school. Some of my friends had a few; all in all, we were fairly stable, but not entirely so.

My decision to become celibate came from what I was learning at church. I was obviously involved with my children's father, but I had never really dated. He and I moved to Atlanta, where I started going to my current church and learning about how to live holy.

Before that, I didn't know you weren't supposed to be doing what we were doing. As I learned, I knew I needed to implement what I was hearing. So I asked my children's father to move out.

I wanted us to do things right, but my request offended him. He didn't agree and didn't like the fact that I now considered myself single. I learned that if you're not married, you are single. There is no in-between status. So with these decisions, the relationship ended, and I was single for real.

At first I thought he was going along with this idea. Things changed shortly, however. Because we had been together so long and already had kids, he didn't see the point of going through this process. He said the church claimed they wanted families to be together, yet they wanted us to live in separate houses.

The truth is, he wasn't ready to get married and he was looking for excuses. He knew the Word. This proved to me that if you know the Word, but don't apply it, it won't do you any good. He didn't take the Word seriously enough to live it. (See James 1:22-24.)

At first I compromised, saying, "Maybe you don't have to move out, as long as we don't do anything." But the temptation was there, so I changed my mind and told him he had to leave.

Some tough times followed. It took two years before I felt emotionally stable and "over" being single. I no longer needed to hang onto a man just to have someone there. Instead, I got to know who I was and what I needed to do. I discovered that God sees me as being worthy. Once I knew that, it was easy for me to be single.

I've been celibate now for six years and I'm currently not dating anyone. I had an interest in a guy, but he wasn't saved. We knew each other from high school and he heard that I was single. We communicated and then got a little closer. God knew it wasn't a good situation and He ended it quickly. I'm glad I can trust Him that way! (See Proverbs 3:5.)

That was as close as I came to being pursued during my journey to celibacy. I learned that when you are saved, people are attracted to the change in you. That doesn't mean they are changed.

The guy who pursued me made it known that he didn't worship anyone. He said he believed in God, but would not worship a man (he believed Jesus was only a man, and not God). Until he said that, we hadn't talked about religion, but I felt like I needed to bring it up.

God used the situation to make things clear for me. At first, I was disappointed but then I realized that this man was on a different level from me. I would not have been able to share the real me with him because of it.

No one is pursuing me now, probably because I don't go out enough. God revealed that I didn't have the faith to believe He would bring me the right man. I thought I was fine being single, but I really wasn't. It was just that I didn't believe He had someone for me.

Psalms 37:5 says: "Commit your way to the Lord, trust also in Him, and He shall bring it to pass." When I thought about that, I realized God was right. I did not trust Him to bring me a man I would like. I used to be a very visual person; I had a certain rugged type in mind. God informed me that I needed to change my type and change the way I see people.

I learned to stop looking at the visual and start looking at who a person really is, including his personality, goals, and character. Once I started doing that, I was attracted to more people. I was not necessarily physically attracted, but I saw people in a new light.

Now I see with a more mature set of eyes; I don't want to weed out everyone without getting to know them first. I had already seen this firsthand with my children's father. I'm not saying I should have been with him. I'm just saying that I did not realize he had such a sense of humor until after I got to know him.

Through this whole process of getting to know myself, I have learned that I can have male friends who are just friends. I used to think that every male who smiled at me did it because he liked me. A lot of guys thought the same thing when I smiled at them. But that wasn't the case. People can be friendly without being interested in that kind of relationship.

Another thing God has been showing me is that His purpose for my life will match the person He has for me. He hasn't yet shown me that I'll be getting married, but I wrote down all my gifts, talents, and passions. It helps me to see how I might fit well with someone who is lacking in those areas.

For instance, I'm soft-spoken, so someone who is more assertive would be a good balance. I know that I'm very talented in teaching, implementing training and self-help projects, and disseminating information. I think that is why God has brought me to ministry. I can see how I would be of help in those areas.

For now, I'm just waiting to see what God has for me.

Boundaries

The dating process will be very interesting, because I have never dated. Yet I do have some general knowledge when it comes to boundaries.

- First I will find an accountability partner and let this person know what's going on in my life. I would want this partner to check in and make sure I'm being transparent. That is especially important because I have never before been in this position.

- I will avoid being alone with a man after a certain time.

- I already stay away from certain things on television. I can't watch dating shows because I end up thinking about being in a relationship or having someone pursue me.

- I won't bring my date to my house. I have kids at home, and believe it may be a year before I even tell them I'm dating (you never know what will happen in that year's time).

- An "iffy" thing for me is kissing. While kissing is not necessarily a bad thing, I know it could open a door that I don't want opened.

It will be interesting to see how all this works out. It will definitely make being single a lot more real. Sometimes I think about what Paul said about the advantages of being single. He said single people can more easily focus on the Lord (see 1 Cor. 7:32). (I think being married may have some advantages, too.)

Even with boundaries in place, always be aware of your thoughts. If you don't have peace about something, then don't do it. If you have to question it, just let it go. It might not be a bad thing, but it might lead you to something potentially bad. Take kissing, for instance. It might not be bad, because everything God created is good. But it could be used the wrong way.

The same is true of drinking wine. Someone else might be OK with it, but I'm not. That doesn't mean I should tell wine-drinkers they are sinning. It is a personal issue that each one has to deal with.

That is how God deals with us—personally, in every decision that we make. He lets us know, especially with a feeling, when something is not right. Even when the issue isn't described in His Word, He is able to convict us so that we don't do what isn't good for us.

As the Word says, "Don't be wise in your own eyes; fear the Lord and depart from evil. It will be health to your flesh, and strength to your bones" (Prov. 3:7-8).

Check your motive for doing things. One decision can lead to another, and it can impact someone else. You don't want to lead others into wrong situations.

Communication is always important. The stricter a woman's boundaries are, the better it is all around. In my opinion, men tend to bend their boundaries more easily than women do, so it helps when women stand firm.

Advice

When times get hard, find something to keep your mind occupied. Get your attention off the distractions that can cause trouble. God helps me to redirect my attention by doing something like going outside. Especially when my kids were away, I tended to entertain idle thoughts. I had to find something to do, even if it was just getting out of the house. The more determined I was about this, the easier it became.

Even when you set up boundaries, you can end up having sex if you allow your flesh to lead you. I've seen it happen to women I know. Don't allow your flesh to lead your decision making (see Rom. 8:5). We all know that sex is a natural human desire. It is a struggle *because* it's a natural need that we often try to fulfill. We want to satisfy that emotional connection; we just want to have someone there.

Know that you are worthy. Because I have two kids, I felt that I wasn't worthy of being a blessing to someone else. I was wrong; I *am* worthy. My foundation is in knowing that God will provide the desires of my heart and everything else that I need—and He will do it above and beyond what I can think or even imagine (see Ps. 37:4; Eph. 3:20).

Some more pointers:

Learning Scripture is important. Find verses that give you peace; His Word will help you to be OK with your situation. This is something I had to do for myself, and it made a difference.

Emotional stability is the most freeing thing, especially if you have had past relationships. If I had gotten into another relationship, it would not have been good. I needed to embrace some time with myself.

You can do the same! Take it as a learning experience. Learn everything you can about who God made you to be, how He made you, and why He made you. Then just be content with that. Allow God to speak to you in every situation. Look to Him as a person you are in a relationship with. He talks to you all the time; He affirms things about you; and

He tells you everything that is good about you. Psalms 139:1 says, "O Lord, You have searched me and known me."

When God speaks, it's like getting a compliment every single day. If you allow Him to be that someone who loves you, you won't feel a void that must be filled by someone else. It took me a little while to understand this at first, because I was emotionally unstable (especially because my ex got into another relationship soon after we broke up).

Don't look at someone else's situation; just focus on yours. Emotional stability is what I prayed for every second of every day. I prayed and believed that God would do it. I never realized the extent to which He would do it! Now things are totally opposite to what they used to be. Now, if I see my ex and he talks about his girlfriend, I don't have to do or say something dumb.

My advice is simple: Just cherish your relationship with God. *He* is your man first. The psalmist wrote: "The Lord is my shepherd; I shall not want" (Ps. 23:1).

God is *your* shepherd, too. The more you realize that He provides and loves you, the bigger the shoes the next man in your life will have to fill. Your future husband will have to meet his role of going to God and providing for you, knowing that God has openly provided for you all this time.

Uheri's "No Sex, What's Next?" Checklist

- Achieve emotional stability.
- Learn who you are while you are single.
- Allow yourself to be in a relationship with God.
- Allow God to be your man.
- Find an accountability partner.
- See people on a deeper level. Check out a man's character, not just his physical appearance.

- Keep your mind occupied. Distract yourself from the distractions.

- Know that you are worthy because God says you're worthy.

- Know that God will fill any and every void in your life.

Message from God

My child, your Daddy has great things for you. Never think that you don't deserve My best. Nothing from your past has stopped Me from wanting to give you the very best that I have for you. You are My child—royalty in every sense of the word. Therefore, you will have what the royals have, which is nothing less than perfection. Your children are blessed. You are blessed. Your future is blessed. Your husband is blessed. All these things are blessed because they are all in Me. You are seated at My right hand with Christ Jesus. You deserve what He has. You will have what He has and much more. You will do great things for the kingdom. Things you haven't even thought of yet. Daddy is smiling!

God Knows You, Specifically

Chapter 7

$\mathscr{A}$LIZA:

EVERYONE IS PROMOTING SEX

WHAT DO YOU EXPECT KIDS TO DO?

"Honor marriage, and guard the sacredness of sexual intimacy between wife and husband. God draws a firm line against casual and illicit sex" (Hebrews 13:4 MSG).

My Story

I was watching a Christian television show I normally don't watch. This particular episode piqued my interest. The main character's son was going off to college and all the men in the family were telling him to make sure he had some condoms.

That is a problem! Why are they promoting sex by telling him to make sure he has condoms? Nothing in the Bible tells us to make provision for sin or the continuation of sin. The Word is very clear: You can either repent of your sin (renew your mind, change your lifestyle, and turn away from sin), or you can die in your sin, because "the wages of sin is death" (Rom. 6:23). Those are the only two options you get. So while this show promotes ungodly sex, I will promote the FAITHFULNESS needed to adhere to God's commands and stay pure.

I'm Aliza. I'm thirty years old and have been celibate for six years. It seems like there is a common thread with fathers not being at home; that's my story, too. Only God knows why he wasn't there. The funny thing is that he remarried, had more kids, and now takes care of that family. I can't even begin to explain why that is and how he chose which kids he would care for and which ones he wouldn't. He had another child close to my age and provided child support; but he wouldn't send my mother anything for me.

That wasn't the only strange detail. There was a two-year period when I stayed in Houston with my uncle. My father lived a couple of apartment complexes down from us, so I would get to spend time with him. I thought it was interesting that between the ages of six and eight, I stayed with my uncle, but only visited my father.

All of this was factored into my decision to have sex at the age of fourteen. Because I had no father in my life, I dated older guys, never guys my own age. God showed me that I was looking for a father's love in them.

When I first had sex, I didn't like it. I didn't understand why guys felt so pressed to have sex. All I would do was lie there. Not until I tried to give it up did I start to enjoy it. Then I saw myself as boy-crazy. I couldn't see myself being with just one guy, and I definitely couldn't see myself married. Guys were just the emotional attachment I used to fill a void I didn't even realize was there. It meant a lot to have someone tell me I was beautiful and wanted.

I have now been born again for ten years. I hadn't grown up in church, but when I started going to church I went to church alone because my mom was always working to take care of us. Once I decided to change my lifestyle, it took me a while to become celibate. The enemy was playing with my mind.

Then God showed me that I had value. I remember reading in Scripture about one of David's sons who was in love with his own sister. He was madly in love with her, but once he had sex with her, he began to hate her. (See Second Samuel 13:1-15.)

That passage helped me to see how this happens in life today: a man says he loves you, he has sex with you, and then he hates you.

My decision to be celibate stemmed from my relationship with God. I realized that you can't say you love Him and live the sort of lifestyle I was living. You will only feel ashamed. Plus, I didn't want to be a hypocrite. So, at the age of twenty-three, I started my journey to celibacy.

To me, celibacy means that I have a relationship with God, and there is no other option. It's different from being abstinent. Abstinence has more to do with campaigns to prevent AIDS and STDs.

Celibacy results from your relationship with God, so that you won't be ashamed or disgrace the name of Christ. There is real meaning behind it. It's different from the world's message about waiting until you fall in love. How many times will you fall in love? They don't say wait until you get married—just wait until you fall in love so that you can share that "special moment" with that "special person." This goes to show that you cannot get your morality from the world. You definitely cannot get it from a television show!

It's amazing how, when you really know God, He gives you peace and value that make you stand out in a crowd. When I'm dating and men find out how long I've been celibate, they always ask, "How do you do it?"

It's simple. I don't want to disappoint God. I want to be "fully pleasing Him, being fruitful in every good work" (Col. 1:10).

I understand now that you have to have a sense of self-worth and value, so that when a man comes along who only wants sex, it's easy to tell him to keep it moving. I think it's different for most guys. When they say they are celibate, many of them are still masturbating, watching porn, and having oral sex. They say they are celibate because they are not having intercourse.

It's not that way with me. I'm not doing any of those things—no masturbating, watching porn, touching myself—nothing. I'm all the way pure.

Now I go through dating spurts. Sometimes I have a surge of dates. Other times I'm "on the island" all by myself. When I date, I tell guys straight up, "I'm not sleeping with you."

These days, when I think about sex, I'm wishing I could be with my husband. When I first started on this celibacy path, I was physically burning because I wanted sex so badly. But that feeling has lessened over time. I still desire to have sex and I still look forward to it, but the burning has stopped.

At times I have had very vivid sex dreams to the point where I think the sex is really happening. When I wake up, I rebuke those dreams in the name of Jesus, because sex is only for the purpose of marriage.

I always say, "Lord, if godly men and women don't find their mates, what representatives of godly marriage will the earth see? Gays are getting married. Strippers find two or three husbands. Lord, I just want one."

It almost looks like the world's way is winning. I have coworkers who don't know how to be godly, yet they are married. So many women don't know what it means to be a godly wife and mother, yet they are married and have kids. Sometimes I think, "I am doing it God's way, wanting to have kids and wanting to be married, yet I'm just sitting here twiddling my thumbs."

But God is saying not to be "weary while doing good, for in due season we shall reap if we do not lose heart" (Gal. 6:9).

Boundaries

It's very important to have boundaries. Boundaries can separate the right guys from the losers. They also help you maintain your relationship with God and eliminate any wrong options that might surface.

My boundaries are pretty simple. Here is what I tell potential dates:

- We might kiss and hold hands, but that's it.

- You're not going to stay at my house past 10 P.M. We will not be alone together in my home at that hour.

- We will not stay out late.

- We will not watch romantic movies at home.

- We can't be talking on the phone at one or two in the morning, unless you have a night job. (I have learned that we are more sexually aware at night. The conversations start with, "Awww…you're so pretty. What are you wearing under your pajamas?" You don't need those conversations. Just go to sleep!)

Advice

I believe some women who really love God and are celibate compromise after a while and have sex with guys so they won't be left alone.

You have to realize that a man like that doesn't love you anyway. The man who loves you won't disrespect your body like that. Knowing this should help you in your walk because you realize true love isn't the motive. Think of it: how many men are you going to sleep with before you get married? I have read about how so many married women fall into depression because they remember their past sexual experiences.

When you're celibate, you can hold your head high. You no longer have to walk into a room full of people worried that you have slept with one of them. The journey is not easy, but it is well worth it. There are certain things you can't look at or listen to. There are certain people you cannot afford to have as close friends. If they are having sex, they can only hinder your walk, not help it.

If you are with a guy who wants to have sex, he will eventually break you down, and you will have sex with him. Don't play those types of games. If you compromise with oral sex, you *will* fall. I used to play those games; I always came out on the losing end.

Understand that sex is not love. Sex never made me feel whole. I would have side effects that made me feel sad and guilty, even before I came to Christ. Love is different from sex. It doesn't leave you broken the way sex outside of marriage does.

My final thought would be to parent your kids so that they don't go down the path you may have walked. My mom never said, "Don't have sex." She would say things like, "If you have sex, you will end up pregnant." It wasn't the right message.

If you aren't talking to your kids, someone else is. Television shows promote sex and birth control. They aren't telling kids to wait until marriage. I will never tell my kids it's OK to get birth control and condoms—not even my boys. It seems parents are more lenient with boys, but why? In our house, it's going to be the same message for my son and daughter: "Wait till you get married."

I have never understood how parents both inside and outside the Church allow their children to have contraceptives. I think they are more concerned about being embarrassed by a child's unwanted pregnancy. I've even heard some parents say, "My kids can have sex at the house, because at least I know where they are."

That's foolishness. My kids will know from the very first day that they are getting ready for a husband or wife, not a boyfriend or girlfriend.

Aliza's "No Sex, What's Next?" Checklist

- Teach your kids to get ready for a husband or wife, not a boyfriend or girlfriend.

- Value yourself.

- Understand the purpose of marriage, family, and sex. Then teach it to your kids.

- Look to God for love, not man.

- Know that celibacy is a relationship with God.

- Desire to be married.

- Set boundaries and keep them. It will separate the right guys from the losers.

- Hold your head high because, with God, you are always loved.

- Allow God to make you godly.

Message from God

My child is different from the rest. She is unlike anything I have created. My valleys, brooks, and streams flow from the sound of My voice. My daughter also listens to the sound of My voice. She follows Me, and in her I am well pleased. She doesn't listen to voices on the right or the left. She is My sheep and she definitely knows My voice.

Continue to follow My will and My way and I will continue to guide you to all truths. I am the way, the truth, and the life; just follow Me. I will make your way prosperous and let no harm befall you, for you are My child. You are the one that I love, so you rest safely between My shoulders. I call you blessed, My child, because you are a partaker in Christ Jesus. You are My beloved. Continue to listen to Me with your heart and I will continue to pour out My words to you. I will continue to show you goodness and mercy all the days of your life—because you listen to Me. You are a wonder, a sight to behold.

God Wants a Relationship with You

Chapter 8

*R*OSALIND:
THERE ARE HOT GUYS
AT CHURCH...

BUT NO ONE IS MAKING ME STUMBLE

"For you were once darkness but now you are light in the Lord. Walk as children of light" (Ephesians 5:8).

My Story

I never did know how to deal with emotions. Even as a child, I bullied others. It was my way of feeling secure and becoming popular. My life was not the way it looked to others. My father didn't spend any time with me. Instead, he used to "buy me" with stuff. People saw the material things that I had; but they never saw me crying in my mirror asking God, "Why did You put me here?"

I was broken and could not find my way, so I created one for myself. If only I had known that GENTLENESS would get me further in life than being mean could. I am still working on that one; I'm not the way I used to be, but I still have a ways to go.

My name is Rosalind. I'm twenty-eight years old and I have been celibate for nine months. I used to be the kind of girl who made endless demands. It was my way of compensating for the attention I needed but never got from my father. So I demanded attention from everyone else. That was how I operated from grade school to college. You either gave me what I wanted, or I bullied you or cut you off. It was one of the three.

Even though my father didn't live with us because he was re-married, he was always in the 'hood. But we had no real relationship with him. That is where my own lack of communication started. I saw how he spoke to my stepmom: *he didn't.* He was silent most of the time. He wouldn't come around to see us; he would just send us money. He bought all of us the way he bought me.

My mom, whom we lived with, was there but she was busy working, so my sister and I did a lot of things on our own. We went to church on our own and got baptized on our own. There was a church right next door to us, so we would leave the house and be at church. We never blamed our mother for being so busy because we understood that she had to work and support us. Still, it wasn't right.

There was a lot going on during my youth, but none of it was the real reason I decided to have sex. I had sex because I wanted to. My mother was very strict, and living with her was not always easy. If I had any kind of ache or pain, she would immediately take me to the doctor. What she really wanted was to make sure I wasn't pregnant.

That irritated me. When I got to college, I wasn't under my mother's rules anymore. I knew I could do whatever I wanted, and that's what I did.

On my twenty-first birthday, I had sex with my college boyfriend at the time. Because I did not have an emotional connection with my parents, I never felt an emotional connection in my adult relationships. After I had sex with my boyfriend, I didn't want to talk to him anymore.

My friends said I did him wrong, but that was the way I saw life. I dated guys without having any emotional connection to them. The truth is I didn't really like sex at first, so I didn't want to have more of it. As far as I could tell, I wasn't very good at it anyway.

Over time, I gained experience and began to enjoy sex more. A certain guy I dated allowed me to awaken my emotions. Most guys had a "give me what I want and move on" mentality. This was different. For the first time, I experienced some emotion, and even started to fall in love. I'd never had to deal with that before, so I did not understand exactly what was happening.

We weren't in a real relationship; we were just having sex, at least as far as he was concerned. In my mind, it was going deeper than that. My emotions were getting tied into him, and I wanted a real relationship. I didn't know how to handle it. Instead of communicating, I lashed out at him.

It hurt when everything between us fell apart, but at least I was aware that I had emotions and had to deal with them.

Other relationships followed that one, but none was quite the same. Finally, I decided to become celibate, because I was tired of doing things the same way. A year later, I was still going to the clubs, but not feeling like I belonged there anymore. I complained about the smell of smoke in my hair, and I wanted to leave those places almost as soon as I arrived.

At the time, I didn't understand what was happening. Now I know it was because my spirit was being called to God. It took a year, but I came to Him. My coworkers had been inviting me to church. They felt like God could bring me the person I needed if I would just go to church. My mentality was: "I'm good like I am. I don't need church." After fighting it, I decided to go to church anyway.

My life has not been the same since! God is really working on me and getting things straight in my life. I know I couldn't be in a better place right now. I even met up with an old friend in church. What a small world it is! God brings people together so we can learn and grow in an atmosphere where we are all on the same page, learning about God.

Right now, I know I'm not ready to date. I don't want to mess up anyone else and I want to preserve what God is doing in my life. That doesn't mean that I don't look. We do have some hot guys at church, but none have made me stumble. I am keeping my focus on God and the plan He has for my life. Nothing else matters. I know that if I continue to follow Him, He will direct me on the right path. All I have to do is stay connected with Him.

Boundaries

Being new in Christ, boundaries are especially important. If that is where you are, boundaries will make it much easier to stay on track. God will guide you every step of the way.

My boundaries are simple:

- I tell guys, "You can't come to my house, and I'm not going to yours. If you want to see me, you can take me out and spend some money."

- No nighttime phone calls! I tell guys, "Look out your window. If it's dark outside, don't call me."

- It's important to avoid people from the past. If you don't want to go backward, leave them behind.

- Having an accountability partner is key. This person won't always say what you want to hear, but it will help keep you on track and accountable.

Stick to your boundaries and don't bend. If anyone does anything to threaten your boundaries, that person is not for you. Just move on.

Advice

I can't give too much advice as this journey is still new to me. One thing I can say is, "Be transparent." Open yourself up; talk to others, and let them help you. If I were in your life, I would be the one to ask enough questions to get to the root of the problem. Then I would try to get you whatever help you need to get free. I would give you some scriptures to stand on, and I would keep praying for you.

We would be learning the "dos and don'ts" of celibacy together. We would walk through the highs and lows, the great days and the not-so-great days. (I haven't had any bad days yet!)

For my part, I'm staying in the Word. It *really* helps me. I have about twenty scriptures on my mirror that relate to what I'm going through. Because I'm new with reading the Bible and being involved at church, just about everything in Scripture touches on what I'm going through.

I love the Word. It is truly my daily bread. I know that if you will get into the Word, God will speak to you. He will even speak when your Bible is closed and you are doing things around the house. He will use every opportunity to reach you. All you have to do is listen.

One thing I would say for sure: know your worth. Know that God created you and has given you something worth holding on to. No matter what your past looks like or what you did yesterday, God forgives you and still loves you. His Word says: "If we confess our sins, He is faithful and just to forgive us our sins and to cleanse us from all unrighteousness" (1 John 1:9).

Don't allow your situation to put a limit on God's love, because His love exceeds all things (see Eph. 3:19). You have value in Christ Jesus, and you are important. You are fearfully and wonderfully made by God (see Ps. 139:14).

Once you tap in to His power, your life will change. You will not look at guys the same way you did yesterday. God will give you a fresh pair of eyes. You will see men for who they really are. This will make it much easier for you to make the right decisions—no more wasting your time, energy, or money on the wrong relationships. God will be your "Man in the middle"; He'll tell you when to invest in a relationship and when to move on.

God is our Father, and that's what good fathers do for their baby girls!

Rosalind's "No Sex, What's Next?" Checklist

- Find yourself an accountability partner.
- Run to God.
- Embrace God.
- Know that He is God.

- Take off the armor. It's time to be transparent.

- Allow God to heal you.

- Embrace the people God has placed in your life.

- Don't run from change. Embrace it.

- Seek His face, because He is seeking yours.

Message from God

It is OK to open up. You don't have to fight this battle alone. I did not put you here to be by yourself. Share your life with those around you. These are your brothers and sisters in Christ. Allow them to be that shoulder you cry on, or the one you call when you just need to talk to someone in the middle of the night. I am here with you, but I provided people for you as well. It's time to break any strongholds in your life. Allow My goodness and gentleness to surround you. No longer do you have to hide from people. No longer do you have to keep things from people. Let them in. This is what you asked for, so embrace it…cultivate it. Sow good seed on good ground and watch your harvest grow. Don't sow seed on stony ground because it's a waste of your time. You can keep that seed to yourself. It's time to awaken to the blessings I have for you. It's time for you to accept them. Just know that it's time. It's a new season for you, but you have to embrace it. Don't run from others, run to others. They are here for a reason.

God Will Comfort You
in Your Time of Need

Chapter 9

Yori:
To Sin or Not to Sin?

That Is the Question!

"Flee sexual immorality. Every sin that a man does is outside the body, but he who commits sexual immorality sins against his own body" (1 Corinthians 6:18).

My Story

Not to sin. That is the answer! But it is easier said than done when your body wants what it wants and ignores what your heart is saying. You have probably heard from some of the other ladies who never allowed sex to overtake them completely. Well, that's not my story. I went too far because I lacked SELF-CONTROL.

It's only by the grace of God that I am where I am today. First John 1:9 states:"If we confess our sins, He is faithful and just to forgive us our sins and to cleanse us from all unrighteousness."

That is confession made easy! If we have sinned against the Father and we repent, He will forgive us and make it as though it never happened. But repenting has to be heartfelt. We have to cry out to God, admitting that we have stepped outside His will and are sorry for it. It means actually turning away from sin to change our whole way of thinking and living in regard to that sin.

We repent, and He forgives. That is great news. But the most important part is to make it a lifestyle change. It's not just about being sorry but continuing in the same acts because you know you can repent and be forgiven again. He loves us. There is nothing we can do to make Him love us any more or less. Still, we don't want His wrath on our lives.

My name is Yori, and I am thirty-two years of age. I have been celibate for two years since God called me back to Him. I fought that call for a whole year; but He kept calling me, because He had a plan for me (of which I was unaware).

Exactly a year after He told me that sex was off limits, I fell. Thankfully, He didn't allow me to fall so hard that I would go back to what I came out of. He just reminded me that I am living for a purpose now and it is time to stand back up and finish the race.

That's what I did, and I haven't looked back since. That is not where my story began, however. There are reasons why He started calling me in the first place.

I was raised in a two-parent household. My mother married my stepfather when I was about two years old. Although my stepfather was the only father I had ever really known, I did know who my biological father was. He lived about thirty minutes away from us but would only come around when there was a death in the family. I could count on seeing him at funerals, but I could never be sure when I would see him otherwise.

That hurt me badly. It wasn't until I got older that I realized just how badly I was hurt by it. I always sought the father-daughter bond I never had growing up. My stepfather was an excellent provider, but I started to see him as less of a daddy and more of a provider. He would give us things, take us out to dinner, teach us about how guys think, and take us on family vacations. He seemed to be doing everything that a father should do for his kids, but there was something missing. To me, it seemed like he felt obligated to do these things because he was married to my mother. I didn't think he really wanted to do them. Our relationship is better now. But as a teenager, there were a lot of emotional issues I had to deal with alone.

There was a lot of physical abuse between my mother and step father, although more of it was on my mother's side. To get away from the chaos, I would run away to the house of whatever boy I was dating at the time. I was very suicidal during my high school years, because I felt like no one wanted me, especially not my father.

When sex was introduced into my situation, I used it as another means of escape. My first time was when I was sixteen, a month before my seventeenth birthday. My friends had been talking about sex and how good it felt. They said I should go ahead and try it. They even used a banana to demonstrate how to put on a condom.

Although my friends stressed having "safe sex," I should not have been taking advice from people who had already decided to have sex outside of marriage.

In any case, I fought their advice and my hormones for a year. Then I gave in and decided to have sex with my high school sweetheart. The first time wasn't what I expected at all. I heard that losing my virginity would hurt and might cause some bleeding. None of that happened with me. The guy I was with didn't even believe it was my first time, because the "normal" things didn't happen.

After another try, those things started happening. It seemed as though this sexual experience opened a door that should have remained locked until marriage. Once I got started, I felt like I couldn't stop. Even though I had sex with only one guy throughout my high school years, sex became more of an addiction than anything else.

I would skip school or be at his house after school. I lied to my parents about where I was, and was generally disobedient. My attitude was not good: I didn't care about getting in trouble because nobody knew where I was anyway—at least not until they started reading my journals.

I was a kid who liked to write. I wrote books and stories and journaled about my life. When my mother and stepfather found my journals, things changed. The sex didn't stop, but relationships became broken.

After a year of college, I felt I had to get away from it all, so I joined the military. While serving was an awesome experience, it also played a big part in fulfilling my sexual desires. Being away from home with no real adult supervision was something I enjoyed; but it wasn't what I needed.

The freedom to have sex with whomever I chose—without having to hear my parents' carrying on about it—made me want to explore this sex thing even more. I was always a person who educated myself on everything. Whatever I was interested in, I would read books until I was an expert. Sex was no different. I had plenty of books about almost anything related to the sex act. I also had partners to practice on. Sex became my boyfriend, someone who was with me every single day.

Then I met a certain guy who was the sum total of all the guys I was messing with at the time. I gave up all the other guys, and we became exclusive. The sex was better than I'd had with any of them, so it was easy to walk away. There never had been an emotional connection with them anyway.

With this new guy, I had what I thought was a win/win situation: great sex and the emotions to go with it. The relationship lasted for about eight months. Then, because of my emotional issues and my inability to get to the next level in a relationship, we broke up.

It was the hardest thing for me. I really loved him, but I didn't know how to move past the point of it being just about sex. The next step was foreign to me. I tried talking to him about moving forward, but he thought I was trying to break up with him. So we ended things.

Within the next six years, I had my daughter, and my thinking started to change. I wanted a future with her father, but because of his actions with other women, we ended it.

My mind went back to wanting emotionless sex. I met a guy who introduced me to a world I had no idea existed—the world of swingers. As a single parent, I did everything for my daughter's sake; but I had this other life on the side.

Being able to have sex whenever I wanted and as much as I wanted seemed perfect to me. The availability increased my appetite and fed my addiction so that I felt like I really could not stop. My whole day revolved around having sex. It was ridiculous! I even researched classes on sexual addiction, because I wanted to stop but didn't know how.

Because I had my mom and sister living with me at the time, my daughter was always looked after, even when I went out. Then God started calling me. A lot of things around me were falling apart. I know now that it was because of my disobedience. I was living the life the devil wanted me to live, and I was getting his results—destruction. I was tearing down my own life when God said, "That's enough."

From that point forward I stopped having sex—cold turkey—and became celibate. When God does something, He does it big. To go from having sex every day to not at all could only be God.

He started telling me that I was going to get married. In my mind, I was taking care of my daughter and getting my career together; I was not thinking about marriage. Then God started speaking through my daughter, who was only three years old at the time. She started telling me that I was getting married and having twins. It shocked me, because it was coming from her. But at that point, I knew I had to listen, so I started getting my life right and going to church.

The next year, I got saved and baptized. Although I grew up in the Church and was baptized at a young age, I didn't know what it meant. I thought it had to do with belonging to a specific church. Not until I got older did I realize what salvation was. I knew I had to do it the right way—with understanding. Even so, change has been hard; but it's nowhere near as hard as where I came from.

When I became celibate, I didn't know what to expect, but I knew it was something worth doing. I remember being so sexually frustrated at one point that I wanted to pull out my hair. I was reading the Bible, meditating on Scripture, and going to church regularly. For me, it didn't make sense. What was I missing? I prayed to God saying that, if He wanted me to be celibate until I was married, He would have to take the desire away from.

God knew where I had been. He knew why the desire was so strong. Now I needed to understand it. I paced back and forth talking to God.

I cried because I didn't want to go back to where I came from. But I didn't know how to put my feelings under subjection.

Needing help, I spoke with my spiritual mother and let her know what I was going through. She said she went through the same thing, and told me I could do it. In my mind, she was married and did not realize my plight. I needed to hear this from someone who was single and didn't have a man to go home to.

I said, "God, I need to hear from You. Tell me what to do." At that moment, my spiritual mother offered to loan me a DVD called *No More Sheets* by Juanita Bynum. It made a huge difference in my life. Hearing about how she went through the same things I was going through helped to decrease my urges significantly.

Now, when strong urges come, I can look back to how I got through it when I thought I was going to fall back to my old ways. The path of celibacy requires work and diligence, but it yields great rewards.

Boundaries

My boundaries are different from the norm. I didn't have clear-cut boundaries because God had already been working on me for three years. Besides the one guy with whom I slipped up, I hadn't been on a single date.

Later on, after inviting a man over to my house, God told me I needed some clear boundaries. Nothing sexual happened, but the guy stayed overnight, and I knew that was a bad idea.

God speaks to me in dreams, visions, and pictures. He was so kind to draw me a picture that gave me the guidance I needed. In the picture, there were five boxes. One box on the right side of the picture was labeled *Friend Box*. Three boxes were lined up on the left side. Each had its own label: *More Than Friends, Relationship,* and *Engagement.*

At the top center of the picture was a box labeled *Marriage*. If you could see these boxes drawn as I saw them, it would look like you were walking down an aisle. He told me that if I followed His directions in regard to His boundaries, I would get to walk down the aisle to marriage.

What I thought was that I would decide which box each guy belonged in, based on my feelings for him. God said no to that idea and then explained how He intended the boxes to work:

- *The Friend Box:* Everyone starts off here. No one goes in any other box without God's permission. The Friend Box can only be locked by two people: God and the guy in question. If I decided to lock the box based on my emotions, I would not be following God's will for my life. Once that box is locked, that's it. The person in the box will never be more than a friend, because the box cannot be reopened. (You do have a free will, so be careful about deciding to lock this box on your own.)

- *The More Than Friends Box:* A guy can move into this box if he is not locked in the Friend Box. In this box, you get to know who he is—his likes, dislikes, character traits, background, etc. This is part of finding out whether you share a connection beyond physical attraction. At this point God will either confirm that the man is just a friend, or He will move him up to the Relationship Box.

- *The Relationship Box:* This box is smaller than the first two because not many people advance this far. Once a guy's likes, dislikes, character, and background are known and God approves, he moves to this box. Now you and he are seeing each other exclusively. This is the time to decide whether you can live with each other's character traits, annoying habits, family, and lifestyle for the rest of your lives. Anything can happen at this point: The man in question (or you) could decide not to pursue the relationship further. Then he would return to the Friend Box. If the decision is made to pursue the relationship, he would go on to the Engagement Box. That determination would be made by a sort of trinity: God, the man, and you.

- *The Engagement Box:* This box is even smaller than the first three because, if you are listening strictly to God, only one man will get to this box. At this point, marriage has already been considered a "go."

- *The Marriage Box:* This is the ultimate goal. The box looks like a jewelry box for a wedding ring. This is where the "trinity" has decided to enter the union as husband and wife.

God set strict boundaries to be followed before a guy could be placed in any of the boxes:

- No men are to come to my house. I am too comfortable there, and I am liable to go too far when I feel at home.

- I am not to stay at a man's house past 8 P.M. During the day is fine. My hormones don't really awaken until it is dark outside.

- No talking after 10 P.M. That's when my sexual side starts to wake up and make demands. It is better for me to be sleeping by that time or reading a good book. The telephone will definitely get me into trouble after a certain hour.

I know that if I follow God's boundaries for my life, I won't fail. I want to continue on this path until He introduces me to my husband and we say "I do." Falling would be detrimental; but I have to remember that God is always there to help me stand back up if I do fall.

There have been times on this journey when I came close to falling. I was following God's will for my life and really not seeing anyone who was attractive to me. That is, until I saw *him.* He was gorgeous. Everything that I liked physically in a guy, he had. I would try to talk to him every so often. He would speak, but it wasn't full-on conversation. So I was ready to move on.

Then God said, "Get to know him."

I was shocked. With the exception of a strong, "No, he's not the one," God had never talked to me about a guy before. So I obeyed and started on a journey to get to know this one. One evening, I invited him over. We watched a movie, and it got physical. He left the next morning and God immediately gave me a set of boundaries.

Did I follow them? No. I really was into the physical at that time, and because I hadn't felt the touch of a guy in so long, my body was awakened by his—to the point that I thought about sex and got aroused. My body would physically burn because I wanted to have sex so badly.

Many times, I ended up at his house and he ended up at mine, kissing and touching and just being physical. God would talk to me while I was on my way over to his house; I would make excuses the whole way there. After a couple of months, I knew I had to stop. I couldn't go into the next year being disobedient.

I really tried not to pursue this person any longer, but my body had other things in mind. I didn't know whether or not he was my husband, but God had said that he would be in my life for a lifetime. After a church-wide fast, my urges were gone.

His weren't. I thought not seeing him for a couple of weeks would curb both our sexual appetites, and at first it did. But a couple of months later, the kissing, touching, and movie nights started up again. God always convicted me about the situation. I really wanted to stay on the path God set for me, but I was allowing my flesh take over and make my decisions.

Today, things are a lot better because I haven't been in those compromising situations with him. My mind is renewed, my body is no longer physically burning, and I'm waiting on my husband to arrive. This guy and I are just friends now. I know that's the foundation God wanted for us the whole time. It was just our flesh wanting our relationship to be something more.

I kept asking God to take the desire away from the both of us. I also asked Him to take this guy away, but God said, "You have to deal with this temptation. If you can't handle saying no, how will you say no when you get married? Your husband might not be there twenty-four hours a day. Saying no now will let Me know whether you are indeed ready to get married."

It made so much sense. I must admit I got too close with this guy; but once I became adamant about being spiritually married to my future husband and not wanting to disappoint him or God, I've kept more distance. Like a friend told me, "You will engage in a sin because you like it. You will stop when you don't."

That is so true! I no longer enjoy the sin of my past. I only look forward to the future God has promised.

Advice

Set boundaries and keep them. Not keeping them was my downfall. I allowed my flesh to run the show and I almost fell for the devil's suggestions, which is exactly what he wants. It's up to us to recognize his voice and immediately send him away. We then need to occupy our minds with something else. Being physically active always helped me—whether it was walking, running, or going to the gym. I had to do something active to keep my mind and body separated from the desire for sex.

Stay away from people who make you weak. Both saved and unsaved guys will challenge your boundaries, because guys generally like to challenge rules. That's not true of *all* guys, only the ones who want what they want and will press for it.

If a guy is challenging your boundaries, it is better to stay away from him or limit certain conversations with him. If guys or even gals in your circle are talking about having sex, you would do best to avoid them and stay by yourself. Get some new friends. Get an accountability partner, too.

I have an accountability partner, and I used to tell her things after the fact. I'm learning to tell her before anything happens, so she can build me up and check in on me. I might not want to hear her advice because I already know what I should or shouldn't do. But she is there for a reason, and God definitely talks to her when He knows I'm up to something. She's always there to help me stay on track.

This road is not easy, but God is with you every step of the way. He knows you can't go through this battle alone. You will need His help if you want to succeed in keeping yourself pure in His eyes. His riches and glory are for you. You just have to want them for yourself.

Understand that no matter what your past looks like and which parent wasn't there for you, God is always there for you. You came through your parents but you came from God. He will never leave nor forsake you (see Heb. 13:5). If it is in His Word, it has to come to pass.

There are a lot of things I have done in my past because I was looking for love and attention from a father who wasn't there. In the midst of my looking, my father passed away. That's when I felt really lost, because I didn't know how to put all my unresolved issues to rest.

I went looking for love in all the wrong places. Eventually, I even got to the point where I was no longer looking for love; I was just looking to fulfill my sexual desires, and wanted nothing more to do with my sexual partners.

But God! He came and took away all the voids in my life. When I found God, I felt like I had four or five holes in me. When I sought after Him earnestly, I could literally feel those holes closing up. It was the best feeling I'd ever had, and my life hasn't been the same since.

Yori's "No Sex, What's Next?" Checklist

- If you are not saved, it's time!

- Realize that your parents' past treatment of you should not dictate your current actions.

- Understand that God has a bigger plan for your life than you can see.

- Set boundaries and keep them.

- Put your emotions in check.

- If it doesn't feel right, don't do it.

- Find an accountability partner.

- Surround yourself with positive, likeminded people.

- Understand that guys always go into the Friend Box first.

Message from God

I am a Father to the fatherless. I never intended for My children to grow up without a mother or a father. I have been here the whole time. My sheep know My voice. As long as I am your Shepherd, you will never be in want. The shadow from the valley will try to make you feel as though it can harm you, but it can't, because I am with you. Your God is here to supply all of your needs. "I am the vine, you are the branches. He who abides in Me, and I in him, bears much fruit; for without Me you can do nothing" (John 15:5).

Mount
St. Celibacy

On the other hand, the path to Celibacy will start off rocky (renewing the mind), it will be hard to climb (finding people on the same path and getting an accountability partner), and you may have to lighten your load as you head to the top (get rid of soul ties, emotional baggage, and people), but once you get to the top, you'll be ready to SOAR like an eagle.

TRANSPARENCY

It's been three years, yet I'm still going.
But I wonder why, because she's still flowing.
She used to run me, back in the day,
I would meet a guy and want to go all the way.
In the bedroom, from him, was all I could need
Because strong sexual desire was all I needed to feed.
All those emotions and feelings were what I would dread
And when that time came, on his nightstand a letter read:
"It was cool while it lasted, but I have to say
My time here is over, so you have a nice day."
I was never that female, who wanted to stick around
I mean my dad never did, so I was always ready for the next round.
But then the day came when I heard someone say,
"Enough is enough, for you. There's a better way."
He lifted me up and dusted me off,
Placed me on the path of righteousness and whispered real soft,
"You are fearfully and wonderfully made.
No longer will you be looking for a quick roll in the hay.
See, what I have for you is beyond measure.
Because you, My child, are a great treasure.
I will find a guy for you, who's a good fit.
So all the others, as of today, you can quit.
I'm your Father, no longer do you have to search
For someone to heal, in you, past hurts."
So that was my past and now in the mirror I see
The image of my Father. Now, that's transparency.

(Written after coming to Christ)

What's Next for You?

Each of the women you have read about has decided that the road to celibacy is far better than the road to instant gratification. Every step of the way they have relied on their heavenly Father and the fruit of the Spirit of God—Love, Joy, Peace, Longsuffering, Kindness, Goodness, Faithfulness, Gentleness, and Self-Control—to continue the walk to higher ground.

There is an important first step in any life journey: to receive Jesus Christ as your Lord and Savior (see the prayer, below). Without Christ in your heart, this journey will be very difficult. But if you allow Him to guide you on this path, He will make it both possible and glorious, just as it is written:

> *Are you tired? Worn out? Burned out on religion? Come to me. Get away with me and you'll recover your life. I'll show you how to take a real rest. Walk with me and work with me—watch how I do it. Learn the unforced rhythms of grace. I won't lay anything heavy or ill-fitting on you. Keep company with me and you'll learn to live freely and lightly* (Matthew 11:28-30 MSG).

Celibacy is not an easy road to take, but with the help of God, your accountability partner, and the principles already outlined, the road will be a lot easier than if you did it on your own. In fact, you *can't* do this on your own. God is right there with His hands stretched out, ready to help you. But you have to want that help for yourself. He is not going to force it on you. We have been given a free will to choose what we want. Even when choose sin, He is merciful to forgive us and cleanse us from all unrighteousness—if we will confess and move forward with Him (see 1 John 1:9).

So, what is next for you? What can you learn from these women's stories? What can you implement today? What soul ties do you need to break? Which path will you choose today—instant gratification or celibacy?

Know that if you choose the path to celibacy, you are not alone. God will guide you through the path less traveled, if you allow Him. He will gladly take you to that ultimate finish line.

I hope you have enjoyed these very personal stories and can utilize these beneficial principles to help you on your journey through celibacy. And remember—get it right, keep it tight, until your wedding night.

If you are not saved and are ready to take that first step on a successful journey into celibacy with Jesus Christ, the Word says you only have to believe with your heart and confess with your mouth and you will be saved (see Rom. 10:8-10).

So, let's do it, together, now! Believe in your heart and say this prayer with me:

> *I believe that Jesus is the Son of God. I believe He died for me on Calvary's tree and bore my sins for me. I believe He rose from the dead and is alive right now. Dear Lord Jesus, come into my life, now! Come into my heart now. I believe with my heart. Therefore, I say with my mouth that Jesus Christ is my personal Lord and Savior. And I am, right now, born again.*

Congratulations! You have made the ultimate life decision. Your life will never be the same again. The angels are rejoicing with you right now in heaven. God will direct your path. All you have to do is call on Him for help and listen for His directions.

Your next steps are easy:

- Find a good Bible-based church, so you can fellowship with other believers.

- Pick a prayer time to speak with God each and every day.

- Make time, each day, to read your Bible.

God will never give up on you, so don't give up on Him. The devil will always try to throw a wrench in your plans. He is your enemy. His name is satan. Once you understand this, you will know exactly where the opposition is coming from when it arises.

You will never be without help. You will always be able to call on God and He will fight the battle for you. God doesn't like anyone messing with His anointed children. Just read Psalm 18 in its entirety, and you will see what I mean. God will come down from heaven with a mighty thunder to deal with those who hurt you.

Allow Him to handle vengeance for you. You need not (and must not) do it yourself (see Rom. 12:19). Just know that you are with God and He is with you. What can anyone do to you while you are in the Master's hands?

The answer is, absolutely nothing!

So no longer do you have to look at your past and where you have come from. All those things are old and passed away. You are now a new creature in Christ Jesus. (See Second Corinthians 5:17.) He will direct your path from this moment on. Just tune in to Him. He loves you, and so do we.

> *And you were dead in your trespasses and sins, in which you formerly walked according to the course of this world, according to the prince of the power of the air, of the spirit that is now working in the sons of disobedience. Among them we too all formerly lived in the lusts of our flesh, indulging the desires of the flesh and of the mind, and were by nature children of wrath, even as the rest. But God, being rich in mercy, because of His great love with which He loved us, even when we were dead in our transgressions, made us alive together with Christ (by grace you have been saved), and raised us up with Him, and seated us with Him in the heavenly places in Christ Jesus, so that in the ages to come He might show the surpassing riches of His grace in kindness toward us in Christ Jesus. For by grace you have been saved through faith; and that not of yourselves,*

it is the gift of God; not as a result of works, so that no one may boast. For, we are His workmanship, created in Christ Jesus for good works, which God prepared beforehand so that we would walk in them" (Ephesians 2:1-10 NASB).

*If there are more pressing issues that may cause you to be unable to follow these principles on your journey through celibacy, and if you really need help beyond and outside of this book, please contact the appropriate local help centers with any questions you may have.

If Only It Were a Dream

Parables for Real Life

An important aspect of this journey is the willingness to listen to God and His direction for our lives. He is always speaking, although it is sometimes difficult to distinguish His voice from our voices or even the devil's. The more connected we are to Him, the clearer His voice becomes, and the more easily we recognize it.

God speaks to us in many different ways including through dreams, visions, the Bible, and even other people. He also speaks to His people using parables, which are stories with a message.

Many people have dreams and visions but fail to take them seriously, because to their minds, the dreams and visions don't make sense. If we realize and understand that God is actually speaking to us through these means, we will receive the direction God is giving us for our lives, and we will know exactly where He wants us to be.

God often speaks to me through parables that illustrate the key points He wants me to grasp. I know Jesus taught through parables during His earthly ministry, because many of His parables are recorded in Scripture.

Parables are powerful; the narratives stick in the memory and remind us of what God is saying. I believe they can help us today. We definitely need direction from God as we travel the road of celibacy, so I am about to share the parables that have helped me. Pay close attention as you read them. You might even become aware of parables God has revealed within *your* dreams.

The Parable of Results

This dream was so vivid that it felt like I was actually living it. In the dream, I was sitting in the doctor's office when a woman came in wearing a white coat. The room was cold and eerie, and there wasn't much light.

The woman handed me an envelope. When I opened it, I read the words "HIV positive." I fell to the floor crying out, "This can't be right. You have made a mistake. Check it again. Check it again!"

But the woman said, "We didn't make a mistake. You made a mistake. The choices you have been making in life are mistakes you should not have been making."

I went into a panic, my heart racing. Then I woke up, still crying and feeling like I was having a heart attack. That was when God told me, "If you don't change your ways, you are going to kill yourself."

The Parable of Choices

In this dream, a friend and I started off driving or walking, and then ended up walking down a street. I grabbed his hand and said, "Let's go this way."

My choice took us through a bad neighborhood. Once there, I took off running and left my friend behind. He wondered why I ran off, seeing it was my choice to go into that neighborhood in the first place. As I ran really fast, zig-zagging through the streets, he ran after me.

I believe God was saying, "You are deciding to put yourself in compromising positions, but when you get in those positions, you run from them. You know the situations you are placing yourself in aren't good, because you always call out for help when you are in too deep. If you stop choosing those places, you won't have to run through them. Pick a better path."

The Parable of the Pilot

In this dream, I was sitting on a plane bound for an unknown destination. As we prepared for takeoff, I had a conversation with the man sitting beside me—struggling all the while to fasten my seatbelt. Then the pilot made an announcement: "We are trying to take off, but not everyone's seatbelt is buckled."

Still fussing with my seatbelt, I continued talking to the man next to me. Suddenly, I got the clasp closed and we were ready to take off.

I believe God was showing me the following: He is trying to take me somewhere, but I am not ready to go because I am allowing the devil to distract me. If I ignore the distractions and am obedient to what God wants, then I will soar to new heights.

The Parable of Chaos

This series of dreams began with certain family members and me inside a house. When I looked out the window, I saw a car pull up in a creepy way, as if someone was up to no good and staking out the place.

Later, I went back to the window and saw that two people were now out of the car. It was clear that they were plotting how to break in. This freaked me out. So I checked to be sure the door was locked, and took my family upstairs to the master bedroom. I then felt as though locking the front door wasn't enough; I needed to lock every door and window, and even secure the chimney access and any other access points. In the dream, I knew the Holy Spirit was directing me.

This dream occurred on three separate occasions. The third time, it was as if God was showing me what would happen if I left open an entrance to my life. In that dream, I seem to remember opening the door and letting in one person who seemed to be acceptable guest. But that person invited in a few others.

We all sat and talked for a brief moment. Before I knew it, I heard loud noises coming from outside the room we were in. I got up to see what was going on, and realized my family was gone and I was alone.

What I saw next overwhelmed, frightened, and shocked me: In every room of my now expanded house were people I had never seen before. They had broken in and created complete chaos. They partied with abandon and made themselves at home.

I had not seen these people come in, but I now saw what they were doing: everything I owned was being stolen, ripped apart, and trampled upon. Parts of my house were unrecognizable. I could barely believe what was happening, but I understood why. It all stemmed from my giving access to a few, who then provided access to others.

These "people" were really spirits and demonic forces that had been plotting to come after me all along. The ones I recognized and welcomed represented my thoughts of going back to the old ways. That is why we got reacquainted in another room. Then they allowed in other spirits that I didn't know, recognize, or have any idea how to handle. There were many more new spirits than old ones.

It was obvious that I had to take control. Already, everything in my territory had been completely overtaken; but I knew I could not walk away. I went into "beasty mode," screaming at people to get out. I grabbed some and pulled out others from their hiding places until I had thrown out every last one. It completely exhausted me, but I did regain control.

Once they were gone, my place seemed empty. Everything I had worked so hard to get had been demolished so effortlessly.

Now I felt all alone. The truth is that God was there with me. Still, there was a lot of cleaning up to do. There were holes in the walls. Dirt and trash were flung everywhere. Goods were damaged. Debris from the demons' brief presence was strewn about me.

By the time the dream ended, I had gotten God's point. I understood what happens when demonic forces are given entry. Even the slightest opening makes way for chaos to overtake your life. God was telling me to keep all entrance ways closed at all cost, so the devil and his demons will never be able to get in and wreak havoc again. (They cannot enter without permission.)

Leaving doors ajar and windows unlocked is not an option. Having substandard, unsecured access points is not an option, either. Before these dreams, I thought I could rekindle certain "dangerous" areas of my life and still be in control of the rest. That idea was simply a product of self-deception.

The Parable of Connection

In this parable, God showed me an Internet connection. I saw the main computer and the Internet with a bright red "X" between the two. Every once in a while the red "X" would appear and I would lose my connection to the Internet. Then the red "X" would go away again, my connection would be restored..

God explained that I was the main computer and He was the Internet. He said that if I did not stay connected with Him by reading and meditating on his Word, going to church, and being obedient to His instructions, then I would not be connected to Him: wouldn't hear His voice as clearly.

When I am on track with God, I have full access to Him. When I waver in following His ways and His instructions, disobedience (the red X) blocks my connection. God is trying to give me everything that I desire, but I have to stay connected to Him in order to receive it.

The Parable of Prayer

This lesson from God did not come by way of a dream, but from my daily prayer time. I had been trying to pray in tongues more, knowing it allows my spirit to communicate directly with the Spirit of God.

During prayer, I concentrated so much on spending a certain amount of time praying in tongues that I lost my focus on God Himself. But the more I prayed in tongues and allowed my mind to get unfocused, the more I heard from God. As He spoke, I became so engaged in the conversation that I completely lost track on time. When my alarm went off, it startled me. I looked up, silenced the alarm, and prayed a little longer.

I believe God was telling me that His blessings work the same way. If we continuously look for them, we can miss out on what God is trying to do in our lives. But if we focus our attention on Him, blessings will show up—blessings so big they will startle us when we least expect them!

The Parable of Flying

When I was younger, I often had dreams in which I flew through the trees far above everything. God showed me that I wasn't of this world. *Normal people don't fly*. But when you are with Christ Jesus, you can soar.

Eagle or Hummingbird?

The eagle does not flap its wings violently in order to fly. In fact, it uses very little effort to reach its destination. It is a privilege to watch an eagle glide across the sky, riding the thermal updrafts which lift it high in the air.

The eagle is smart: it lets warm currents do all the work, even taking the bird to altitudes of ten or fifteen thousand feet and carrying it at speeds of seventy-five miles per hour. The eagle is an expert at going with the flow!

As women, we must learn how to go with the flow of God. If we are guided by Him and allow Him to take over our lives, two things will happen: He will bring us into His best, and He will help us to soar to greater heights than we could ever reach on our own.

Unlike the eagle, the hummingbird flaps its wings exhaustively, between forty and eighty times *per second*. Imagine: in the time it takes you to say, "One," the hummingbird has flapped its wings, on average, sixty times. Some say that, during courtship, the hummingbird flaps even faster. Why? Because it is trying to make things happen.

We women often act like hummingbirds. Instead of soaring and going with the flow, we flap around violently trying to make certain things happen. We need to stop doing that—it only gets us into trouble. We can trust God to take over and teach us how to soar.

The Parable of the Movie Theater

In this dream, I went to the movies alone, not sure of what film I was about to see. I remember walking through the lobby searching for anyone who looked familiar, but I recognized no one.

When I looked up to see the title of the movie, I saw none. I proceeded to my seat anyway, and God started the film. It was a compilation of clips from my childhood. As it played, I thought I was the only one in the theater, but in what little light there was, I saw that other people were there, too.

At the end of the dream, God showed me the number nine, which represents finality or judgment. I believe He was revealing that the movie was the finale of my past life.

What I believe He is saying to women everywhere is this: When you choose the walk of celibacy, you might feel as though you are walking alone. You might even get to the point of feeling like you are in the dark. You won't see the light at first, but then it will appear. The light is God, and He will guide you where you need to go. He will even fill up your life with people you can call when times get hard.

While you chose celibacy on your own and decided to break away from the world to follow God, He will make sure that you are never alone. He will also make sure that light surrounds you. He will be there even when all you can see is darkness.

The Parable of the Feathers

In this dream, I walked into a building and the doors shut behind me. In front of me was a gorgeous staircase, glittering with gold sparkles. I felt very happy as I looked at it.

As I walked up the staircase I saw feathers the size of people, standing close together. The feathers were beautiful and of various colors. It was as though they were waiting for me to reach the landing above me. As I drew closer to them, I felt a sense of calm, as if everything was going to be alright.

I believe God was showing me that I am in His house now. The world was outside the doors I had just walked through; but the doors were now shut. Then God said to me, "You are about to walk into your blessings."

God's house is filled with gold. The feathers spoke of everything being light from this point forward, as long as I follow God. I had arrived at the place I'd always heard about but never saw. Neither did I know anyone else who had arrived there. Having reached the place, I understood that I was royalty and it was time for me to receive my blessings.

The road to celibacy can lead *you* to the same results. If you trust God and His plans for your life, your journey will be light. Scripture says His yoke is easy and His burden is light (see Matt. 11:29-30).

Allow God to guide your path. With Him, you are never alone.

What Would Jesus Do?

Jesus would do what His Word says! In these final pages, I have compiled scriptures that I believe will strengthen and encourage you. Please use this list as a handy reference, even memorizing passages that will sustain you in the days to come.

Use this list often, but keep reading your Bible. That is what Jesus would do.

Scriptures

Genesis 1:27-28—"So God created man in His own image; in the image of God He created him; male and female He created them. Then God blessed them, and God said to them, 'Be fruitful and multiply; fill the earth and subdue it; have dominion over the fish of the sea, over the birds of the air, and over every living thing that moves on the earth.'"

Genesis 2:18—"And the Lord God said, 'It is not good that man should be alone; I will make him a helper comparable to him.'"

Genesis 2:24—"Therefore a man shall leave his father and mother and be joined to his wife, and they shall become one flesh."

Exodus 14:14—"The Lord will fight for you, and you shall hold your peace."

Numbers 23:19-20—"God is not a man, that He should lie, nor a son of man, that He should repent. Has He said, and will He not do? Or has He spoken, and will He not make it good? Behold, I have received a command to bless; He has blessed, and I cannot reverse it."

Deuteronomy 28:1—"Now it shall come to pass, if you diligently obey the voice of the Lord your God, to observe carefully all His commandments which I command you today, that the Lord your God will set you high above all nations of the earth."

Joshua 1:8—"The Book of the Law shall not depart from your mouth, but you shall meditate in it day and night, that you may observe to do according to all that is written in it. For then you will make your way prosperous, and then you will have good success."

2 Samuel 13:1, 14-15—"After this Absalom the son of David had a lovely sister, whose name was Tamar; and Amnon the son of David loved her....However, he would not heed her voice; and being stronger than she, he forced her and lay with her. Then Amnon hated her exceedingly, so that the hatred with which he hated her was greater than the love with which he had loved her. And Amnon said to her, 'Arise, be gone!'"

Psalms 1:6—"For the Lord knows the way of the righteous, but the way of the ungodly shall perish."

Psalms 19:14—"Let the words of my mouth and the meditation of my heart be acceptable in Your sight, O Lord, my strength and my Redeemer."

Psalms 23:1—"The Lord is my shepherd; I shall not want."

Psalms 37:4—"Delight yourself also in the Lord, and He shall give you the desires of your heart."

Psalms 37:5—"Commit your way to the Lord, trust also in Him, and He shall bring it to pass."

Psalms 68:5—"A father of the fatherless, a defender of widows, is God in His holy habitation."

Psalms 86:3—"Be merciful to me, O Lord, for I cry to You all day long."

Psalms 136:1—"Oh, give thanks to the Lord, for He is good!"

Psalms 139:1—"O Lord, You have searched me and known me."

Proverbs 3:5-8—"Trust in the Lord your God with all your heart, and lean not to your own understanding, but in all your ways, acknowledge Him and He shall direct your paths. Do not be wise in your own eyes; fear the Lord and depart from evil. It will be health to your flesh, and strength to your bones."

Matthew 4:7—"Jesus said to him, 'It is written again, "You shall not tempt the Lord your God."'"

Matthew 5:37—"But let your 'Yes' be 'Yes,' and your 'No,' 'No.' For whatever is more than these is from the evil one."

Matthew 7:1-2—"Judge not, that you be not judged. For with what judgment you judge, you will be judged; and with the measure you use, it will be measured back to you."

Matthew 7:7—"Ask, and it will be given to you; seek, and you will find; knock, and it will be opened to you."

Matthew 11:28-39—"Come to Me, all you who labor and are heavy laden, and I will give you rest. Take my yoke upon you and learn from Me, for I am gentle and lowly in heart, and you will find rest for your souls."

Matthew 22:37-38—"Jesus said to him, 'You shall love the Lord your God with all your heart, with all your soul, and with all your mind.' This is the first and great commandment."

Mark 10:6-8—"But from the beginning of the creation, God made them male and female. 'For this reason a man shall leave his father and mother and be joined to his wife, and the two shall become one flesh'; so then they are no longer two, but one flesh."

John 10:27—"My sheep hear My voice, and I know them, and they follow Me."

Romans 5:17—"For if by the one man's offense death reigned through the one, much more those who receive abundance of grace and of the gift of righteousness will reign in life through the One, Jesus Christ…".

Romans 6:23—"For the wages of sin is death, but the gift of God is eternal life in Christ Jesus our Lord."

Romans 8:1—"There is therefore now no condemnation to those who are in Christ Jesus, who do not walk according to the flesh, but according to the Spirit."

Romans 8:5—"For those who live according to the flesh set their minds on the things of the flesh, but those who live according to the Spirit, the things of the Spirit."

Romans 8:6-8—"For to be carnally minded is death, but to be spiritually minded is life and peace. Because the carnal mind is enmity against God; for it is not subject to the law of God, nor indeed can be. So then, those who are in the flesh cannot please God."

Romans 10:8-10—"But what does it say? 'The word is near you, in your mouth and in your heart' (that is, the word of faith which we preach): that if you confess with your mouth the Lord Jesus and believe in your heart that God has raised Him from the dead, you will be saved. For with the heart one believes unto righteousness, and with the mouth confession is made unto salvation."

Romans 12:2—"And do not be conformed to this world, but be transformed by the renewing of your mind, that you may prove what is that good and acceptable and perfect will of God."

Romans 8:28—"And we know that all things work together for good to those who love God, to those who are the called according to His purpose."

1 Corinthians 6:15-16—"Do you not know that your bodies are members of Christ? Shall I then take the members of Christ and make them members of a harlot? Certainly not! Or do you now know that he who is joined to a harlot is one body with her? For 'the two,' He says, 'shall become one flesh.'"

1 Corinthians 6:19-20—"Or do you not know that your body is the temple of the Holy Spirit who is in you, whom you have from God, and you are not your own? For you were bought at a price; therefore glorify God in your body and in your spirit, which are God's."

1 Corinthians 7:32—"But I want you to be without care. He who is unmarried cares for the things of the Lord—how he may please the Lord."

1 Corinthians 10:13—"No temptation has overtaken you except such as is common to man; but God is faithful, who will not allow you to be tempted beyond what you are able, but with the temptation will also make the way of escape, that you may be able to bear it."

2 Corinthians 5:10—"For we must all appear before the judgment seat of Christ, that each one may receive the things done in the body, according to what he has done, whether good or bad."

2 Corinthians 5:17—"Therefore, if anyone is in Christ, he is a new creation; old things have passed away; behold, all things have become new."

2 Corinthians 5:21—"For He made Him who knew no sin to be sin for us, that we might become the righteousness of God in Him."

2 Corinthians 10:5—"casting down arguments and every high thing that exalts itself against the knowledge of God, bringing every thought into captivity to the obedience of Christ."

Galatians 5:22-23—"But the fruit of the Spirit is love, joy, peace, longsuffering, kindness, goodness, faithfulness, gentleness, self control. Against such there is no law."

Ephesians 1:4—"…He chose us in Him before the foundation of the world, that we should be holy and without blame before Him in love…."

Ephesians 2:1-8—"And you He made alive, who were dead in trespasses and sins, in which you once walked according to the course of this world, according to the prince of the power of the air, the spirit who now works in the sons of disobedience, among whom also we all once conducted ourselves in the lusts of our flesh, fulfilling the desires of the flesh and of the mind, and were by nature children of wrath, just as the others. But God, who is rich in mercy because of His great love with which He loved us, even when we were dead in trespasses, made us alive together with Christ (by grace you have been saved), and raised us up together, and made us sit together in the heavenly places in Christ Jesus, that in the ages to come He might show the exceeding riches of His grace in His kindness toward us in Christ Jesus. For by grace you have been saved through faith, and that not of yourselves; it is a gift of God...."

Ephesians 3:19, 20—"to know the love of Christ which passes knowledge; that you may be filled with all the fullness of God. Now to Him who is able to do exceedingly abundantly above all that we ask or think, according to the power that works within us...."

Ephesians 4:22-24—"...put off, concerning your former conduct, the old man which grows corrupt according to the deceitful lusts...."

Ephesians 5:5—"For this you know, that no fornicator, unclean person, nor covetous man, who is an idolater, has any inheritance in the kingdom of Christ and God."

Ephesians 5:23—"For the husband is head of the wife, as also Christ is head of the church; and He is the Savior of the body."

Philippians 3:12-14—"Not that I have already attained, or am already perfected; but I press on, that I may lay hold of that for which Christ Jesus has also laid hold of me. Brethren, I do not count myself to have apprehended; but one thing I do, forgetting those things which are behind and reaching forward to those things which are ahead. I press toward the goal for the prize of the upward call of God in Christ Jesus."

Colossians 1:10, 11—"that you may walk worthy of the Lord, fully pleasing Him, being fruitful in every good work and increasing in the knowledge of God. Strengthened with all might, according to His glorious power, for all patience and longsuffering with joy...."

1 Thessalonians 4:3—"For this is the will of God, your sanctification: that you should abstain from sexual immorality…."

Hebrews 11:1—"Now faith is the substance of things hoped for, the evidence of things not seen."

Hebrews 12:2—"looking unto Jesus, the author and finisher of our faith, who for the joy that was set before Him endured the cross, despising the shame, and has sat down at the right hand of the throne of God."

Hebrews 13:4, 5—"Marriage is honorable among all, and the bed undefiled; but fornicators and adulterers God will judge. Let your conduct be without covetousness; be content with such things you have. For He Himself has said, 'I will never leave you nor forsake you.'"

James 1:2-3—"My brethren, count it all joy when you fall into various trials, knowing that the testing of your faith produces patience."

James 1:8—"…a double-minded man, [is] unstable in all his ways."

James 1:14-15—"But each one is tempted when he is drawn away by his own desires and enticed. Then, when desire has conceived, it gives birth to sin; and sin, when it is full-grown, brings forth death."

James 1:22-24—"But be doers of the word, and not hearers only, deceiving yourselves. For if anyone is a hearer of the word and not a doer, he is like a man observing his natural face in a mirror; for he observes himself, goes away, and immediately forgets what kind of man he was."

James 4:7, 8—"Therefore submit to God. Resist the devil and he will flee from you. Draw near to God and He will draw near to you. Cleanse your hands, you sinners; and purify your hearts, you double-minded."

1 Peter 1:16—"because it is written, 'Be holy, for I am holy.'"

About the Author

Yolanda Harris is a mother, writer, and advocate for those in need of help. During an evening in prayer, God told Yolanda that He hears the cries of his baby girls and sees their struggles. He said to let them know that they are not alone.

With this book, God found a new way to reach them. Because Yolanda struggled with celibacy, she can relate to women from diverse backgrounds who struggle as she did. Her passion has always been people, so God is using her testimony and the testimonies of those like her to reach the multitudes. God's baby girls are His rewards, and He wants them to know that they are fearfully and wonderfully made. He gives them His love freely and unconditionally. There is nothing they must do to receive His love.

Yolanda currently resides in Hiram, Georgia with her daughter, Madison Bryant. They regularly attend and serve at Faith Christian Center in Smyrna, Georgia.

Yolanda would love to hear from you. Please email her any questions or comments at writer.yolandaharris@gmail.com.